SMALL-GARDEN POOLS

GARDEN MATTERS

SMALL-GARDEN POOLS

PHILIP SWINDELLS

WARD LOCK

First published in Great Britain in 1991
by Ward Lock Limited, Villiers House,
41/47 Strand, London WC2N 5JE, England
Reprinted 1992

A Cassell Imprint

© Ward Lock Limited

Line drawings by Michael Shoebridge

Text filmset in 11/11½ point ITC Garamond Light
by Columns of Reading
Printed and bound by
HarperCollins Manufacturing, Glasgow

British Library Cataloguing in Publication Data

Swindells, Philip
Small garden pools. – (Water gardens).
1. Water gardens
I. Title   II. Series
712.6
ISBN 0-7063-7028-7

CONTENTS

PREFACE

Water in all its guises has long fascinated man. Now with modern materials and technology, a pool, waterfall or fountain can easily be created on the smallest plot. Even if you only have a patio or terrace you can enjoy the benefits of this wonder of Nature.

Whether you are enchanted by the sounds and sights of moving water, its unique reflective quality, or the opportunity that it presents for raising gorgeous waterlilies and brightly coloured goldfish, this book offers the most economical and practical routes to success.

P.R.S.

CHAPTER 1

INTRODUCTION

Stand beside any body of water in a public place and watch the behaviour of passers-by. Almost without exception they will stop or at least glance momentarily. Whether it be moving water or still, planted or lifeless, human beings are inextricably drawn to water. There is little surprise, then, that owning a pool at home has become so popular. Indeed, in the countries of the western world, with the advent of modern materials to make construction easier, pool ownership has become the fastest rising interest in the garden.

WHY HAVE A POOL?

This is the question that the husband usually asks when his wife informs him that he must dig the hole! The wonder of water is difficult to define, but the personal pleasures that can be derived are many. For the keen gardener a pool offers a great opportunity to grow a range of interesting and colourful plants that cannot be accommodated elsewhere – gorgeous, fragrant water-lilies, stately bog irises and unusual submerged and floating aquatics.

Fish fanciers have a wonderful chance to expand their interests. Many of the coldwater fish that are traditionally kept in aquaria prosper in a well-planted outdoor pool. Not only do they grow more rapidly, but they are also more inclined to breed freely. Of course, much of this is associated with the lush growth that happy plants make in an outdoor pool, but equally it is associated with local wildlife which comes in and is often a rich source of food for the inmates. Indeed, wildlife can be the objective of creating a pool. Native plants and native fish can yield a rich and fascinating ecology and it is the garden pools of the nation that are said to be the last refuge of a number of endangered newts and frogs.

Water can be enjoyed for its own sake, though, whether it be a placid stillness that reflects all about it, or a crashing, raging fury. Each has its mystical and wonderful aspect that can provide not only visual appeal, but sound appeal as well. Indeed, water can be used as an art form in the garden – a mirror in the case of still pools, a liquid sculpture when a fountain is playing.

HOW MUCH WILL IT COST?

This is always the most critical question when contemplating a project. It is difficult to provide a hard and fast answer as the diversity of materials for pool construction, together with the wide range of plants and fish available means that it can cost a fortune or it can be done very economically. The best way to establish a pool is with young vigorous plants and small lively fish. These are generally cheaper anyway, the only aspect that detracts from this proposition being the fact that the effect is not so instantaneous.

When contemplating a pool, economy can be satisfactorily made with small sizes of plants and livestock, but quality should never be sacrificed. This is especially important when deciding on the construction of a pool, whether it be a liner or pre-formed shape. Economy in the purchase of a poor quality pump is equally a recipe for disappointment. Well manufactured products will last a lifetime with sensible use.

Time is also a consideration when deciding upon creating a pool. In discussing maintenance in a later chapter it can clearly be seen that this aspect is as economical, if not more so, as any other feature in the garden. It is during construction that the greatest expenditure in time is made. Even a modest sized pool, perhaps 1.8 m × 2.4 m (6 ft × 8 ft) will take the inexperienced person two weekends to construct. Add another weekend to plant and half a day to choose and introduce fish. If an associated rock garden and waterfall are to be added, then another few days will be required. Plenty of time should be anticipated for ancillary work, too, for a pool cannot just be placed in the garden without any disruption. There are usually nearby areas to reorganize and perhaps turf and paving to relay.

THE POOL AND CHILDREN

Garden pools and young children clearly do not mix. Until a child is 9 or 10 years old it is most unwise to consider a pool. Even though the average garden pool rarely exceeds 75 cm (2½ ft) in depth it is a potential death trap for small children. Unlike a swimming pool which is uncluttered by plants, a garden pool is filled with obstacles which can hamper the escape of a small child, even one who can falteringly swim.

Many put forward the proposal of a pool which can be converted into a sand pit. This is rarely a satisfactory arrangement as the pool quickly collects stagnant water. A sand pit requires some form of drainage and while it might be a nice idea for grandparents to fill their pool with sand, they would be better advised to turn it into a bog garden. A pool filled with a richly organic soil mixture can produce a fine display of bog garden plants.

OTHER CONSIDERATIONS

If the question of cost and the potential for problems with children have not dissuaded you from a small pool, take a look at your site. Shortly we will consider the various aspects for the well-being of the plants and fish, together with the design and placing which make the pool aesthetically pleasing. However, there are earlier considerations to be made. Not least of all you will need access for construction and for various services: electricity if you want moving water, and drainage if you wish to be able to empty your pool, and let us not forget that during the summer, water will be regularly required to top up that lost to evaporation.

Access to the site may seem to be a minor point if your pool is to be small, but remember that even from a small excavation there is a considerable amount of soil to be disposed of and easy access for the wheelbarrow is essential. Not only that, but where are you going to put the soil that is removed? In some cases it will need removing from the site entirely, perhaps in a hired skip, so whereabouts are you going to put this for a couple of days?

Water is vital to the enterprise and there should be easy access to a mains supply. While large quantities will not be required, except when initially filling the pool or occasionally cleaning it out, topping up to compensate for evaporation can be a daily occurrence in very warm weather. A hosepipe permanently dragged through borders and across the lawn can be a constant source of irritation, so if possible think in terms of an underground supply, or at least site the pool within striking distance of a tap.

The same applies to an electricity supply, although you will only need this if you intend having moving water or lighting. Even if you have no intention of having either, it is prudent to take account of the proximity of electricity, as during the winter months a pool heater can prove to be invaluable in keeping an area of the pool ice-free, thereby preventing the build-up of noxious gases which can suffocate the fish.

Drainage is also very important. Provision needs to be made for draining the pool periodically, but this need not be elaborate. Many gardeners merely bale out the water on to the surrounding ground and cause little harm. Others, where the pool is higher than parts of the surrounding garden, merely siphon the water off with a hosepipe on to beds and borders, but the more particular pool owner either makes provision with a nearby drain, or in the case of a concrete pond might well fit a drainage plug to a specially laid drain that takes the water away directly.

The greater concern though, is that when the soil water table is higher than the bottom of a liner or pre-formed pool, it can actually lift the pool out of the ground with the pressure of water. With a liner it can cause unsightly 'ballooning'. So any site contemplated for a pool must be properly drained.

If none of the foregoing troubles you, it is time to consider the design of your pool and how it will fit into your garden.

SELECTING A SITE AND DESIGN

A pool is like an artist's canvas, framed and highlighted with plants and enlivened with fish. It is also an ecologically balanced environment which needs carefully contriving if the end result is to be a a happy one. In many respects a pool is unlike any other garden feature, for the essential ingredients are not just the plants, but the way in which they integrate both visually and functionally into the feature alongside other living creatures.

CHOOSING A SITE

It is very important to choose a suitable site for a garden pool, for once installed it is difficult and time-consuming to move. Disturb a pool and it will take a couple of years to regain its balance completely. The placing of a pool is important from the visual point of view, of course, but from a practical gardening point of view it is even more vital. For healthy plant growth to result it is essential to have the pool in an open sunny place. All aquatic plants enjoy full sun, prospering and providing the ideal conditions for a healthy natural balance. An ideal position is not always easy to find, but any situation near trees must be avoided. Not only do trees provide troublesome shade, but falling leaves will contaminate the pool as they decompose, releasing noxious gases.

The practical aspects of a site having been considered, due regard must be paid to the visual. Take a look at nature and you will find that water is always found at the lowest point in the landscape. In a garden, too, water only looks comfortable when placed lower than the surrounding area. It is often the case that the lowest part of the garden is unsuitable because of shade or other practical considerations. When it is so, an effort has to be made to ensure that the soil from the excavation is redistributed in a manner which gives the pool the appearance that it is lower than the surrounding area.

FORMALITY AND INFORMALITY

The overall design of the pool is a matter of personal whim, but to conform to the surroundings a formal setting should accommodate a formal water garden, while an informal garden must play host to an informal pool.

The surface design of a formal pool should rest easily with its surroundings, the shape being of mathematical proportions and consisting of a rectangle, square, oval, circle, or any combination of these. The effect must be one of equilibrium, which extends to the placing of any fountains or other garden ornaments. The informal pool has few rules to abide by as it can be of any shape or size you care to create. For the best effect, though, it should consist of sweeping arcs and curves and not display any fussy niches or contortions which not only look odd visually, but are a nightmare to construct.

Informal water features are often established close to a rock garden. Where possible, the linking of these together to form a single unit is both practically and visually desirable, providing the opportunity for installing moving water with little effort.

Although the overall appearance of the pool in its garden surroundings is very important, the ultimate success of the venture depends heavily upon its internal structure. Plants will not flourish in hostile depths, nor will goldfish be particularly happy. Each group of aquatic plants has an optimum depth at which they will prosper. Most waterlilies and other deep-water aquatics require a minimum of 30 cm (1 ft), while marginal plants should not be expected to grow in more than about 15 cm (6 in). For fish, a minimum depth of at least 45 cm (1½ ft) in some part of the pool is essential if they are all to overwinter successfully. When considering the kind of pool to construct, take into account the purpose that it is to fulfil. Is it going to be primarily a place where interesting plants can be grown, or is it being introduced for its musical or reflective qualities? Once such conclusions have been reached and a decision made about its theme – perhaps a cottage garden look, or maybe an oriental aspect – then consideration can be given to the best method of construction.

This will, of course, depend to a great extent upon the size and shape as well as the placement on the site. We have considered the need for it to be in the open in order that plants and fish prosper and also paid due regard to the fact that it is best located at the lowest level in the landscape where possible. However, at this stage, with a broad theme decided, it is useful to get something down on paper.

If a pre-formed plastic or fibreglass pool is to be the choice then there are the constraints of the manufactured shape which you have mentally to place in position, whereas if the choice is to be a liner or concrete there is greater freedom of expression. Most of us do not have the gift of visualizing the pool in position with its attendant plants. Unless you are one of the lucky few who can it is as well to sketch ideas out on paper.

Relatively few gardeners are artists, and so diagrams quickly become a little out of proportion. In order to get an accurate assessment of the site take one or two photographs of where the pool is likely to be sited and then transfer this in sketch form to a sheet of paper. It is surprising how much simpler it is to get a reasonably accurate view from a photograph than from trying to sketch in the open. It is even possible with a rule to scale trees, nearby buildings and so on, accurately on to the sketch from a photograph.

The pool shape can then be added, together with any nearby plantings. To provide an overview, measure out an area three or four times larger than the actual pond site, use existing features as markers, and transfer the measurements to a sheet of graph paper. The pool can then be drawn in, providing a perspective from above. This simple exercise is vital, especially where a pre-determined pool shape is being used without any facility for alteration on the ground.

Once this has been done, you can go out on to the site and peg out the proposed pool and any adjacent features. This gives a very real feel of how it will be when constructed.

The same procedure should be followed even if the pool is to be a fairly modest affair, perhaps close by the house or on the patio. Mark the area out and see if it is visually acceptable, but also look at the access around it, especially if it is a raised pool. Patio areas can become quite congested, and unexpectedly so when they become host to a raised pool. When looking at how the pool fits in, consider the possibility of moving water. If you plan to have a fountain allow for the fact that the spray may blow about. Be sure that you have made sufficient provision for your guests to sit out on the patio without getting soaked.

CHAPTER 2

POOL CONSTRUCTION

When planning the construction of a garden pool, pay particular attention to the requirements of the various kinds of aquatic plants, for some prefer the shallows around the pool while others require much deeper water. Reeds, rushes and other marginal subjects like marsh marigolds and irises will require shallow ledges around the edge of the pool. These should be about 23 cm (9 in) deep and of similar width if they are to accommodate aquatic planting baskets properly. The depth may seem excessive for plants that enjoy shallow water, but remember that the planting basket will rise the plants' bases close to the surface of the water. Waterlilies and other deep-water aquatics can be positioned in the deeper, central area of the pool. Usually this is at least 38 cm (15 in) deep, but it benefits from being deeper, especially when overwintering fancy goldfish is envisaged.

POOL LINERS

Pool liners are the most popular form of pool construction as they are reasonably cheap and will suit any fanciful shape you may care to design. A pool liner consists simply of a sheet of heavy-gauge polythene or rubber material which is placed in the excavation and moulded to its contours by the weight of water within, finally being secured by rocks or paving slabs placed around the top.

The cheapest liners are made of 500-gauge polythene, often in a bright sky blue colour, and in several standard sizes. These are pre-packed and can be purchased from most sizeable department stores. While being inexpensive, they are the least durable of all, having a life expectancy of little more than three years. Their great drawback is that they perish unless kept totally immersed in water. This in theory is not a problem, but in practice can cause difficulties, for evaporation from the pool surface regularly lowers the water level and leaves a gap between water level and the surrounding ground. This area of the polythene is very susceptible to perishing and general deterioration, and within a couple of years will break up and effectively leave the lower half of the liner detached from the upper part. The most useful purpose to which this liner can be put is as a small hospital pool for fish or a temporary sanctuary for plants when the pool has to be cleaned out.

Pool liners within the medium price range are usually made of PVC, many incorporating a terylene web as reinforcement. They are available in fairly neutral stone and grey colours, as well as bright blue and ornamental pebbledash. These have a much longer life than polythene ones, seldom showing signs of deterioration in the first ten or twelve years, although being vulnerable to mechanical damage and puncturing easily if carelessly managed. While also available in standard sizes, these can often be cut to suit your requirements at little extra cost.

Rubber liners are the most permanent of all and, while not indestructible, are not apparently damaged by sunlight or water after a period of time. Of course they are much more expensive than the other two kinds, but this undoubted durability makes them a better investment when a permanent water garden feature is being constructed. Rubber pool liners are usually black, with a matt finish which provides suitable conditions for some of the clinging algae like mermaid's hair to become established. Algae are generally undesirable in the pool, but when restricted to coating the sides of a pool they are very useful. In the case of the rubber liner they hide it almost completely from view, giving the illusion that the pool is completely natural. For those who must have a vivid blue or green pool special paints are available for use on rubber liners.

WORKING OUT THE SIZE

It may seem fairly obvious that the size of the liner will be substantially larger than the excavation, but it is surprising how much larger it turns out to be. It must be remembered that it is not just the overall depth, length and breadth that have to be considered, but also the overlap of up to 30 cm (1 ft) at the top of the pool for securing it to the ground. If the pool is of an irregular shape, then calculations must be based upon the dimensions of a rectangle which will enclose the most distant edges of the excavation.

The formula for calculating size is (twice the depth + length + 2 overlaps) × (twice the depth + breadth + 2 overlaps).

DIGGING THE HOLE

Before starting to dig it is a good idea to mark out as accurately as possible the size and shape of the excavation. This can be done by taking a length of rope or hosepipe and arranging it on the ground in the desired outline. The surface area and shape can then be ascertained accurately. Never start digging with just a vague idea of how the finished pool will appear, for not only may the pool liner turn out to be of the wrong dimensions, but the overall shape of the pool will quite likely not conform with its surroundings. Also be sure to allow sufficient depth for each kind of plant. Deeper areas of 30–75 cm (1–2½ ft) will accommodate various deep-water aquatics satisfactorily, but shallower water must also be provided for marginal plants, by constructing shelves 15–20 cm (6–8 in) deep, and wide enough to take a small container (Fig. 1*a*). At one point at the pool edge, a very gradual slope could be incorporated so that hapless hedgehogs which fall into the pool would be able to clamber out.

The dug-out hole should be scoured for any sharp objects likely to puncture the liner. Once water is added, the pressure of the liner against the walls and floor of the pool, and consequently against any sharp stone or twig, is such that it can be ultimately forced through the liner. To prevent this happening, it is useful to spread a layer of sand over the floor of the pool and along the marginal shelves to act as a cushion. A similar protection can be obtained for the walls by taking wads of newspaper and wetting them thoroughly before packing them against the walls in paper-mâché style (Fig. 1*b*) Some people use old carpet or purchase soft fleece that is sold for the purpose.

INSTALLING THE LINER

All liners are installed in a broadly similar manner, those made from polythene being spread out on the lawn in the sun for an hour or two before installation in order to become more supple and mould to the excavation more readily.

As polythene liners have little elasticity, they are installed without water being added, but plenty of

a.

b.

Fig. 1 **Construction of pool with liner**
(a) Excavating the hole.
(b) A layer of wet newspaper is used to cushion the sloping
    sides. The pegs allow a spirit-level to be used to check for
    levelness.

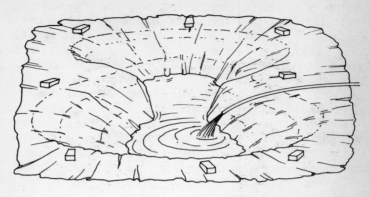

c.

d.

(c) Filling the pool.
(d) Having trimmed the superfluous liner, the pool is then edged either with broken slabs or paving, laid on a bed of mortar.

21

movement should be allowed for, so that, when the water is gradually introduced, the wrinkles can be smoothed out and the liner moulded to the exact contours of the hole. Rubber and PVC liners can be draped across the excavation and weighted down with rocks or paving slabs. As the water is added and the liner tightens, the anchoring weights around the pool are slowly released until the pool becomes full and the liner moulds to its exact shape (Fig 1*c*).

Once the pool is full and as many of the unsightly wrinkles as possible have been smoothed out, superfluous material from around the edges can be trimmed. However, remember to allow sufficient for finally anchoring with stones or paving slabs (Fig. 1*d*). If a less formal edging is desired, there are two other options for providing a neat finish. Providing straight lines are acceptable, lengths of timber can be used and the edge of the liner wrapped around these and secured with wooden lathes. The wood and liner can then be placed just beneath the surface of the surrounding garden. It is even possible to turf up and over the edge. The liner protects the wood from rotting and the whole arrangement means that if alterations or major maintenance operations have to be conducted, finding and securing the edge of the lining is simple. If an informal outline is desired, bricks can be used as an alternative. This is a little more time-consuming to arrange, for each individual brick is wrapped in the edge of the liner and placed against the next. However, it allows great flexibility in making an informal edge.

Once completed, the pool is immediately ready for planting, for pool liners do not contain anything that is toxic to fish or aquatic plant life. The pool liner also gives you an opportunity to do what most other forms of construction are not flexible enough to allow, and that is to construct a bog garden as an integral part of the feature. All that is needed is a pool liner that is larger in one dimension than necessary for the pool itself. This allows the development at one end of a spreading, shallow-pool arrangement 30 cm (1 ft) or so deep which can be readily converted into a bog garden. A retaining wall of loose bricks or stones separates the bog garden from the pool proper and retains a peaty soil mixture. Water from the pool moistens the soil through the barrier, the soil level being just above pool level.

THE CONCRETE POOL

Although hard work to construct, a concrete pool that is properly installed makes a successful water garden. Not only can almost any shape be built, but it is durable and after a couple of seasons begins to look completely natural if correctly constructed. It is vital at the outset to bear in mind the limitations placed upon such a pool by the nature of the materials used, for although almost any shape can be moulded in concrete, it is more sensible to create an excavation that is simple to build.

CONSTRUCTION

When making a concrete pond, the excavation must allow for the thickness of the concrete and at least 15 cm (6 in) of concrete lining should be allowed for. The sides and floor should be rammed and firmed before concreting takes place. Sloping walls that require no shuttering are preferable to sheer sides that demand a complicated struture of boards and supports. So that the concrete does not dry out too quickly it is a good idea to line the entire excavation with builders' polythene before commencing (Fig 2a).

Ideally, concreting should be undertaken in a single day. Certainly no more than 24 hours should be allowed

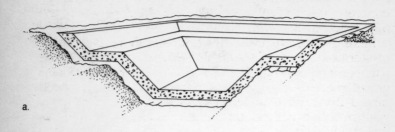

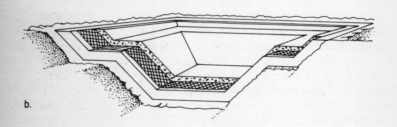

Fig. 2 **Construction of a concrete pool**
(a) A layer of heavy-gauge builders' polythene is used to line the excavation. The concrete is laid to a depth of 10 cm (4 in) over the floor and up the sides.
(b) A final 5 cm (2 in) layer of concrete is then added over mesh-wire reinforcement.

to elapse between joining two areas of concrete or else a potential point of weakness will be created. When a joint has to be made, the surface of the previous day's concrete should have been 'roughed up' to allow the new batch to key with it.

Mixing concrete is hard work, but there is nothing mysterious about it. A suitable mixture consists of one part cement, two parts sand and four parts 2 cm (¾ in) gravel measured out with a shovel or bucket. This is mixed dry until of a uniform greyish colour. When a waterproofing compound is to be added it is done at this stage. There are a number of different kinds available in a readily dispensed powder form. Water is then added to the mixture until it is wet and stiff. A good test of its readiness is to place the shovel in the mixture and then withdraw it in a series of jerks. If the ridges that this produces retain their character then the concrete is ready to be laid.

The first layer should be spread to a depth of 10 cm (4 in) over the entire excavation. Large-mesh wire netting like that used for poultry is then pressed into the wet concrete to act as reinforcement (Fig 2*b*). A further 5 cm (2 in) of concrete is spread over this. This final layer should be carefully smoothed out with a plasterer's trowel. When the sides are steep, form-work or shuttering has to be erected and the concrete poured behind this. Usually of wooden construction, it is vital to paint the surface of the shuttering boards with limewash to ensure that the concrete does not stick and pull away when they are removed. In some cases, merely soaking the timber with water overcomes the problem of concrete sticking to the wood.

When the concrete has been laid, and after any lingering surface moisture has soaked away, the surface should be covered in wet sacks or something similar. Rapid drying out of the surface of the concrete causes hair cracks to appear and these are potential areas of weakness. If the concrete surface area is so large that it is impracticable to cover it with sacks, then a gentle sprinkling of water from a can with a fine rose will provide a suitable alternative. It depends upon subsequent weather conditions, but after a week the concrete should have 'gone off' sufficiently to allow it to be treated with a sealant.

CURING THE CONCRETE

Concrete contains free lime which is injurious to fish and plants in varying degrees. An untreated pool that is filled with water will immediately turn milky and be a most hostile environment for aquatic life. The constant filling and emptying of a newly constructed pool will eventually bring about the remedy, but treatment with a suitable sealant will be permanent. When the concrete is thoroughly dry a product such as Silglaze can be painted on to the surface. This neutralizes the lime and by a complex reaction forms a silica which seals the concrete by internal glazing. Rubber-based and liquid-plastic paints are also useful in preventing free lime from escaping, although their principal role is as a waterproof pond sealant. These paints are available in a range of colours and provide an excellent finish to the concrete pool, but it is important not to neglect the need for a primer. Without this, the entire paint surface will become detached from the concrete like an enormous pool liner. Special primers for these paints are frequently available from garden centres. Being of a clear syrupy liquid they are easily and quickly applied with a brush, but you must ensure that every exposed concrete area is treated.

Once protected against the effects of free lime, planting can take place immediately.

PRE-FORMED POOLS

Pre-formed pools are of two very distinct types: the fibreglass kind and those made from vacuum-formed plastic. The latter are relatively inexpensive and moulded in a tough, weather-resistant plastic. They often have a roughish, undulating finish to simulate natural rock. While being inexpensive and readily transportable, they do have the disadvantage of flexibility which can cause problems during installation. Fibreglass pools, being entirely rigid and free-standing, present no difficulties during construction, but be very careful over the choice of design. Most are made by fibreglass manufacturers with little understanding of plant life and it is often the case that reeds, rushes and irises are expected to become established on a marginal shelf no more than 8 cm (3 in) wide, while the deeper areas of the pool will not have a sufficiently flat floor to place a single waterlily basket.

There are many different shapes and sizes to choose from and most can be obtained in a choice of colours, so it is wise to obtain a selection of catalogues from specialists and weigh up the advantages and disadvantages of each type before making what will undoubtedly be a sizeable investment. You usually get what you pay for and a higher-priced product will generally be of higher quality. Read the manufacturers' descriptions carefully, for some of the smaller pools are really rock pools which are intended to sit near the summit of a rock garden so that water tumbles down a cascade unit into a pool below. These are relatively inexpensive, but are not suitable for most aquatic plants nor for accommodating ornamental fish. Fountain trays are also shallow and likewise can offer little to aquatic plant life, other than possibly a few submerged oxygenating plants. These are the small pools which act as a fountain saucer in a confined space or serve as a receptacle to catch water spouting from a gargoyle. Even if they are deep enough to house a few aquatic plants, it would be unwise to do this, for when used for their proper purpose, water turbulence is such that none but the coarsest and most vigorous aquatics would survive.

INSTALLING A PRE-FORMED POOL

There is a common assumption when buying a pre-formed pool that all that is necessary is to dig a hole to the shape of the pool and then drop it in. Nothing could be further from the truth. First of all, measure the external dimensions and dig a large rectangular hole that allows the pre-formed shape to rest in it with room to spare. It is most important that the excavation is sufficiently large to allow for comfortable backfilling once the pool is in place (Fig 3a). Cover the floor of the excavation with a layer of sand on which to sit the pool, raising the shallow end up to the correct level by means of a temporary support of bricks. The top edge of the pool should be about 2–3 cm (1 in) below the surrounding ground level. This ensures that, when backfilling takes place, the inevitable lifting of the pool leaves it at ground level and not above.

Fill in all around the pool. Throughout backfilling it is vital to ensure that the pool is level from side to side and end to end. This can be readily checked with a length of board stood on edge from one side to the other with a spirit level placed in the middle. When the garden soil is in good condition it is possible to backfill with that. However, it is much easier to use a consistent medium like sand or pea gravel, both of which have the advantage of flowing easily and eliminating any air pockets. This should be firmly rammed to ensure that the pool is well seated. Water can then be added. In the

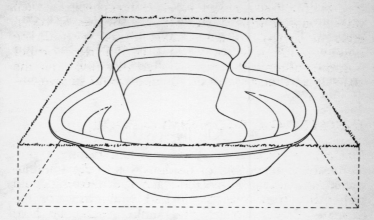

Fig. 3 **Installing a pre-formed pool**
(a) Excavate a rectangular hole that will amply enclose the
    length and breadth of the pool and its greatest depth.

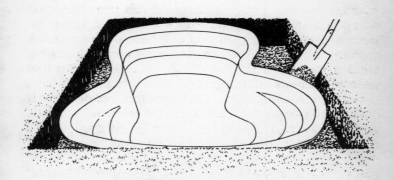

(b) Having checked for levelness, commence to fill the pool
    and, simultaneously, to backfill with sand or sifted soil.
    The water level and backfill level should be kept the
    same to give maximum support to the pool.

29

case of the plastic kinds it is useful to add water as the backfilling is done, so that there is a degree of rigidity (Fig. 3*b*). Providing that the levels are correct from the beginning and water is run into the pool at the same rate as backfilling takes place, there is unlikely to be any problem. Being non-toxic, the pool can be planted straight away.

A POOL IN A TUB

Any receptacle capable of holding water is a potential water garden. Old galvanized water tanks and sinks, or baths with their outlets plugged with putty are all extremely serviceable when sunk in the ground, although some may corrode and leak unless protected initially with a good rubber-based paint. Discarded vinegar and wine casks sawn in half can make the best small pools (Fig. 4). (However, wooden containers that have contained oil, tar or wood preservative should be avoided, as any residue that remains will pollute the water and form unsightly scum on the surface.) No matter what container you use, it is advisable to give it a thorough scrubbing with clean water. Never use detergent for cleaning, as it is difficult to be certain when all traces have been removed. In tanks or sinks where algae have become established, the addition to the water of enough potassium permanganate crystals to turn the water a violet colour will usually have the desired effect.

ADDING A BOG GARDEN

A brief mention was made earlier of attaching a boggy area to the pool when using a liner construction for the pool. The value of this kind of feature should not be under-estimated, for a bog garden knits a pool into the

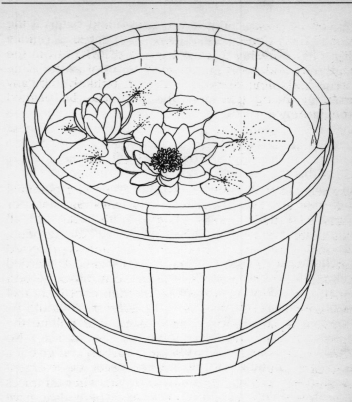

Fig. 4 **Tub garden**
Discarded vinegar or wine casks make excellent small-pool containers when sawn in half and waterproofed inside with bitumen paint.

garden landscape. To look effective, the bog garden should have a similar surface area to the pool.

Even though it is most desirable and natural, a bog garden does not have to be physically attached to the pool. In the case of both concrete and pre-formed pools a bog garden usually has to be constructed independently, abutting the pool. In this case, there is no water filtering into it from the adjacent pool, so it is important that it has ready access to a hosepipe, for in dry spells it is often necessary to raise the soil moisture level.

The independent bog garden can be constructed using a liner, broadly along the lines described earlier. Alternatively it can be made of concrete or a pre-formed shallow pool sunk into the ground, but neither of these latter options is as easy to turn into a bog garden feature, either practically or aesthetically. While it is true to say that the expert in concrete construction can build an excellent structure in which to create a bog garden, the expertise of the professional cannot be easily transferred to the average weekend gardener, for whom attempting such an enterprise single-handed may court disaster.

Whether for a free-standing bog or for a bog attached to a pool the soil mixture should be the same. Plenty of organic matter should be mixed in with the soil before planting. If any fertilizer is to be added, it should be a slow-release kind, like bonemeal or hoof and horn. Indeed, throughout the life of the bog garden any regular applications of fertilizer should be of this kind, although a number of the modern foliar feeds can be used freely without presenting any problem. The soil moisture content should be constantly monitored in an independent bog garden, for in hot weather it can soon become very dry. Regular watering is essential, for although a liner prevents water escaping into the surrounding soil, most bog garden plants have quite expansive foliage which transpires freely.

CHAPTER 3

MOVING WATER

Many pool owners desire moving water and with this in mind manufacturers have introduced a wide range of fountains, waterfall units and pumps to suit most requirements. Cascade or waterfall units made of fibreglass or vacuum-formed plastic are readily available in many shapes, sizes and colours. Some consist of a simple bowl with a lip, over which the water trickles, while others come in sections of varying lengths and shapes which can be joined together to form complex cascades. Installation is simple, as the units merely need setting securely in position and the delivery hose from the pump inserted into the uppermost one, and the waterfall is fully operational.

A fountain can sometimes be incorporated with a waterfall by the use of a two-way junction on the pump outlet, but in most instances the pump is not sufficiently powerful to produce the desired effect. A fountain alone is a much better proposition and, by the careful selection of jets with different numbers and arrangements of holes, some pleasing spray patterns can be obtained. Apart from straightforward water jets, ornaments depicting cherubs, mermaids and similar characters can be purchased, each designed to take a pump outlet so that water can spout from its mouth, or a shell, or any similar object that they might be holding.

Where space is very limited and there is insufficient room to accommodate a waterfall or fountain satisfactorily, 'masks' and gargoyles can be used with great effect. These are usually imitation lead or stone ornaments depicting the faces of gnomes, cherubs or sometimes the head of a lion, and are flat on one side to enable them to be fixed to a wall. Water is pumped up into the 'mask' and spews from the mouth into a pool below.

While all these contrivances give us the pleasure of moving water, we must also think about the plants beneath. Almost all aquatic plants with floating leaves dislike turbulent water or a continuous fine spray on their foliage, so any moving-water feature that is envisaged should be considered for one end of the pool and out of the direct line of choice plants like waterlilies.

CHOOSING AND INSTALLING A PUMP

Most pool owners now opt for a submersible pump. Except for very sophisticated water features submersible pumps of popular manufacture are perfectly adequate. They are designed to operate completely submerged in the pool and are silent and safe. As they are merely placed into the water, there is no need for a complex plumbing arrangement or a separate chamber, as with surface pumps. Generally, such a pump will consist of a cast body containing a motor, although some recent models are made of non-corrosive materials like noryl. An input unit attached to this will draw water into the pump, often through a filter or strainer which will catch any debris and filamentous algae likely to block the pump. The cover of this unit will be removable and the collected debris should be periodically removed.

Above the input is the adjuster assembly. This can comprise a single or double outflow – the latter will allow water to be discharged as both fountain and waterfall. Control can be exercised over both by the flow adjuster screw. In the case of a fountain, a jet with a series of holes in it will be attached to the outflow to create a spray pattern. Different interchangeable jets are available and these will give varying complexities and heights of spray (Fig. 5). When used to create a waterfall, a length of tube sufficient to reach from the outflow to the head of the cascade is attached.

Some submersible pumps have a very small discharge and so it is important to judge the water flow required before shopping around. Most will provide an adequate fountain, but a surprising amount of water is required to operate a satisfactory waterfall. Most manufactured cascade units require an output of at least 1140 litres (250 gallons) per hour to put a thin sheet of water across their width, while 1365 litres (300 gallons) per hour is required to make a continuous filmy flow 15 cm (6 in) wide. If in doubt about the necessary flow, an indication can be gained by using water from the tap through a hose. The output from the hose can be assessed by pouring into a container for one minute. If the amount of water collected is measured in pints and that figure multiplied by 7.5 the flow in gallons per hour can be calculated. It is then a relatively simple matter to assess the flow required down the watercourse.

Installation of a submersible pump is quite simple, for it is merely placed in the water. It is wise, however, to set it on a level plinth and, in the case of a fountain assembly, it is vital that the jet unit be just above the maximum water level. Connection to the electricity supply should be via a weatherproof cable connector on an extension lead. The most satisfactory arrangement is to have the cable connector concealed beneath a small paving slab. This means that the pump can be easily removed from the pool without disturbing the extension cable if maintenance proves necessary. During the winter the pump should be removed and this arrange-

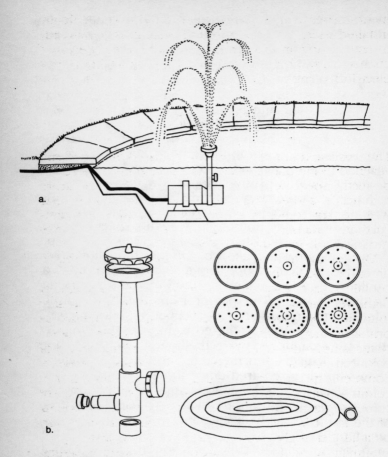

Fig. 5 **Fountains**
(a) A sparkling fountain, achieved by means of a submersible pump, adds the interest of moving water to the pool environment.
(b) Diagram showing how several different spray patterns can be made by means of interchangeable discs at the fountain head.

ment means that a pool heater can be conveniently installed in its place if desired. If a pump is not already in use, clearly an extension cable, with a weatherproof connector, will be required to reach back to the nearest electrical point.

FOUNTAINS

The easiest fountain to install consists of a jet unit attached to the outlet of a submersible pump. These are perfectly adequate for most gardeners, but the more technically appreciative and extrovert among us may wish to try some of the more adventurous systems currently available, especially those that incorporate varying spray patterns or coloured lighting.

One of the most interesting developments in recent times has been the illuminated fountain. This is self-contained and provides a colourful water display at night, yet during the daytime can be used as an ordinary fountain. The addition to the conventional fountain is primarily a spotlight encased in a sealed alloy under-water lampholder unit. This is available with a choice of coloured lenses which give a single colour fountain. Some enterprising manufacturers have also produced a colour changer. This is a revolving disc of different colour segments which automatically changes the colour of the fountain. The rotation of the colour changer can be adjusted to give slow or rapid colour change.

Similar technology is available to provide changing water spray patterns. This is by means of a device which is attached to the pump and which can create up to 18 patterns in a set sequence. Each spray pattern lasts up to 16 seconds while each sequence takes around 3½ minutes to complete. Novel spray patterns can be created with special adaptors that not only vary the height and shape of the traditional fountain, but also produce unusual water patterns. Such an innovation is the bell fountain which, by means of a single adaptor, creates a globular spray pattern, almost like a glass bell in appearance. Single bells are fascinating, but triple bells from a single unit are quite remarkable. Not only are they breathtakingly beautiful during the day, but they can be easily lit at night. A similar feature can be created by the use of a fountain ring. This is a tubular ring with five or more adjustable jets which can provide varying spray patterns. The ring is attached to the outflow of the pump.

The majority of fountains shoot water into the air, but a quite modest feature known as a pebble fountain is most restrained and yet very attractive. Although not technically a fountain, it utilizes the same components as the conventional jet. In appearance it is a contained area of sizeable, attractive pebbles or cobbles through which water constantly bubbles. It is easy to maintain and does not need either aquatic plant life, fish or snails. Essentially it consists of a small concrete chamber which is waterproof and able to accommodate sufficient water to enable a simple submersible pump to operate. A framework of iron bars is placed across the top and this supports fine mesh netting. On top of this a generous layer of washed pebbles or cobbles is placed and the pump outlet drawn up until it is at the surface of the stones. Water bubbles up through the pebbles, creating a cool refreshing effect. As evaporation is rapid, the chamber beneath will require regularly topping up with fresh water.

WATERFALLS

A waterfall is a most attractive addition to a water garden. Usually made from a pre-formed cascade unit of plastic or fibreglass, it is simple to install. All that is

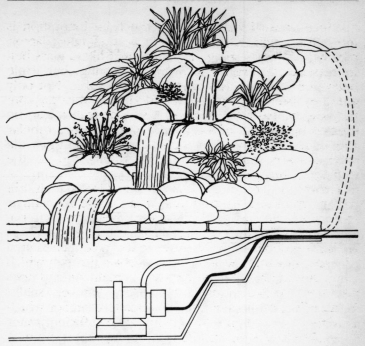

Fig. 6 **Pre-formed waterfall**
Waterfall or cascade units can be made of plastic or fibreglass.
They are simple to install but do ensure that they are level
from side to side.

required is that it is level from side to side and that the
lip protrudes sufficiently to enable the full body of water
to be emptied into the pool rather than on to the
surrounding ground. The hose from the outlet of the
pump is then carefully hidden, but emerges at the
summit of the unit, from which water gently tumbles
down (Fig. 6).

A waterfall does not have to be prefabricated to be
successful and in certain circumstances it is desirable
that it is not. Prefabricated units are not necessarily of

the shape or length desired and, when something special is needed, the waterfall can be made with concrete. Some suppliers suggest that a presentable feature can be constructed using a pool liner, but this demands a considerable amount of skill to achieve satisfactorily.

A purpose-built waterfall will have to conform visually to the site and fulfil its function of delivering water from a higher area to a pool below. The upper part, or header pool, should be at least 15 cm (6 in) deep, but will not be capable of supporting aquatic plant life or fish. Each small basin forming the cascade should be so constructed that, when the water is switched off, a small quantity remains in each. This can be done by tipping the leading edge up, so that water only flows over the lip when a reasonable quantity is being pumped. The concrete used to form the waterfall should be of the same consistency as that used for pool construction (see page 25) and like the pool, benefits from being 15 cm (6 in) thick. While the concrete is still wet, a more natural effect can be created by the addition of rockwork. This can similarly be used around the edges to hide their harshness. It is important that these edges are level in the horizontal plane so that water is distributed evenly throughout each basin.

Waterfalls can be constructed that vary considerably from the traditional form. One of the most interesting of these is the grotto, where a pool is constructed with a background of similar appearance to a rock garden. A small cavern built at the summit contains a pump outlet surrounded by well washed pebbles or cobbles. These stones extend down the watercourse, over which water flows with the aid of a simple submersible pump. The illusion is that the water is emerging from within the grotto. When tastefully dressed with ferns and other moisture-loving plants around its edges, it makes a very attractive feature.

FILTERS

Most pumps have filters attached to their input in order to gather debris and any algae that is likely to cause mechanical problems. Some pumps now have an integral filter which is intended to clarify the water rather than just catch debris. However, it is perfectly possible to fit special filter units to most ordinary classes of submersible pumps in order to extract water-discolouring algae. In a perfect world a pool's natural balance would always be maintained by the various kinds of aquatic plant which act as purifiers and oxygenators and a filter should never be used as a substitute for these. But temporary problems do arise and a filter can undoubtedly assist, particularly in the smaller pool where a natural balance is more difficult to establish.

The pool filter usually looks like a deep tray. It is actually two trays, one inside the other, the inner one containing a foam filter element which is covered with gravel or charcoal. The pump is connected through the outer tray and draws in water through the gravel or charcoal, and then through the filter elements into the pump for discharge as a fountain or waterfall. Debris and algae collect in the medium in the inner tray and can regularly be changed and disposed of. Another system uses a small filter, or algae trap, at the discharge side of the pump. This type of filter must also be regularly changed.

Biological filters are a different proposition. These depend upon the water passing through a gravel or foam medium on which useful bacteria develop. These are capable of converting waste organic matter into plant nutrients. Biological filters operate outside the pool, usually at the summit of a waterfall where they can be suitably hidden. Alternatively they can be placed close by the pool and the water circulated and returned immediately. Biological filters have to be operated continuously for if the filter is allowed to dry out the bacteria perish. Such a filter is not used during the winter; it is just cleaned and put away until the following spring.

INNOVATIONS WITH WATER

Being adventurous with water need not mean that you have to purchase a ready-made package. There are all kinds of things that you can do yourself if you are of a practical turn of mind. This applies particularly to fountain arrangements. One of the most imaginative uses a series of bowls and a conventional fountain spray. Water is pumped up a tall central stem and then tumbles into a small bowl. Beneath this are bowls of the same shape and construction, but of increasingly greater diameters. When the first bowl has filled, the water falls into the second and so on until it reaches the pool below. To ensure that the gently twisting curtain of water falls evenly from around each rim, it is absolutely essential that each bowl is level. The problem created by such a feature, however, is one of excessive turbulence in the pool below. To countract this, one must consider growing few plants other than the all-important submerged oxygenating plants, or else arresting the turbulence by placing beneath the fountain a large ring which is of greater diameter than the lower bowl. Plants can then be grown in the relative peace of the perimeter.

Waterfalls can be exuberant, too and one can scarcely get more exuberant than a water-staircase. Beloved of French and Italian nobility for years, this feature can be tastefully recreated in the small garden. The idea behind a water-staircase is that it appears as a staircase of sparkling, silvery water. This can be achieved by the use of sizeable concrete drainage pipes set in a bed of concrete one behind the other, each pipe slightly above the next. One then has a staircase with rounded steps, but to disguise the edges it is necessary to fill the hollow ends of the pipes with concrete or soil and disguise them with plants. If the pipes are new, they may require treating with a pool sealant.

The effect of a water-staircase can be marvellous, but only when sufficient water is flowing over it. If such a feature is envisaged, do not skimp on the purchase of a pump of sufficient size. The whole concept depends upon the volume of water being sufficient to provide a generous covering of water.

CHAPTER 4

PLANTING THE POOL

Waterlilies and other aquatic plants are ideally planted during the spring and early summer. This is not always possible, especially if pool construction has not started until the spring; planting may then have to be delayed until late summer. While the plants are still actively growing they can be successfully transplanted. The problem is that at this later season the plants are rather unwieldy, untidy and need cutting back quite severely. It is not until the following spring that they start to look respectable again.

CREATING A BALANCE

Establishing and maintaining a balance within the pool is very important. Unfortunately, few pool owners fully understand what this means and how it can be achieved. One of the greatest misunderstandings is that if the pool is well oxygenated the water will always remain clear and balanced – therefore if a fountain is introduced to the pool it will be a cure for all ills, because the water droplets falling into the pool pick up oxygen on the way down. The droplets will be well oxygenated, it is true, and on warm sultry days the fish will delight in their cool spray, but the presence of oxygen is no guarantee of water clarity. This misconception has been inadvertently created because it is submerged oxygenating plants which have the greatest influence on the condition of the water. However, it is not the oxygen that the plants produce which creates clear water and a healthy balance, but the competition that the plants provide for the green water-discolouring algae which invade the pool as soon as the water is warmed by spring sunshine. Algae are primitive forms of plant life and flourish in water that is rich in mineral salts. Only when competition for these mineral salts is provided by more sophisticated plants is there any chance of algae being controlled. When there is sufficient underwater plant growth to utilize all the mineral salts that are present, then the water will be clear. Only when there is an abundance of plant foods available will algae and submerged plants live alongside one another.

Surface shade also helps to reduce the occurrence of algae. It is undesirable that the entire surface of the water is covered with foliage, but for an even balance to be achieved at least a third of the surface area should be covered either with the floating foliage of waterlilies or free-floating aquatic plants. In assessing the area to be covered, ignore that occupied by the shallow marginal shelves and then aim for one third of the remainder to become colonized. When calculating the number of submerged oxygenating plants, required, allow 10 bunches per square metre or one bunch for every square foot of surface area. Most submerged plants are sold as bunches of cuttings and the formula assumes this typical plant material.

PLANTING

All aquatic plants, with the exception of the floating varieties, require careful planting. This can be directly into soil spread on the pool floor or else in properly designed containers. The wise pool owner will always go for containers as much more control can be exercised over plants grown in this way. They can be easily removed for inspection or division, and on occasions when the pool needs to be cleaned out. Specially manufactured waterlily baskets are the most suitable containers to use and are readily available from most garden centres and pet shops. They are made of a heavy-gauge, rigid polythene or plastic material and of a design that will not easily become over-balanced. As they have lattice-work sides, it is advisable to line them with hessian before planting, to prevent any compost spillage into the water, especially when the soil is rather light.

The most suitable compost to use for aquatic plants is good clean garden soil from land that has not recently been dressed with artificial fertilizer. This should be thoroughly sieved, and care taken to remove twigs, pieces of old turf, weeds, old leaves, or indeed anything that is likely to decompose and foul the water.

The soil having been prepared, a little coarse bonemeal can be added. Allow about a handful for each basket to be planted and mix it thoroughly into the compost (Fig. 7a). In recent years specially prepared composts for aquatic plants have become available. These vary widely in quality, but the more popular brands seen in garden centres are likely to be perfectly adequate. The compost to be used should be dampened so that when squeezed in the hand it binds together, yet is not so wet as to allow water to ooze through the fingers.

When planting waterlilies it is advisable to remove all the floating foliage just above the crown. This may seen rather drastic, but it usually dies anyway, and when planted intact the leaves often serve as floats, giving the plants buoyancy and lifting them right out of the baskets. The fibrous roots should also be cut back to the rootstock and any dead or decaying area pared back

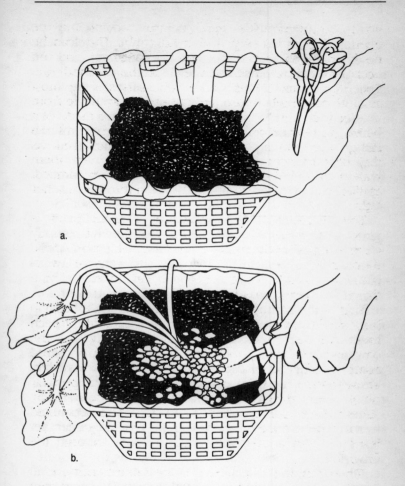

Fig. 7 **Planting waterlilies**
(a) Half fill the basket with soil/compost and trim off the
    excess hessian liner.
(b) The lily is planted firmly in the soil/compost, which is
    then covered with a layer of pea shingle.

with a knife to live tissue, the cuts dressed with powdered charcoal or flowers of sulphur to help seal the wound and prevent infection. If a rootstock takes on a gelatinous appearance and is evil-smelling do not let it come into contact with sound varieties. These symptoms are a certain indication of infection with waterlily root rot (see page 83).

It is important when planting that the compost is packed as tightly as possible into the container. If not it becomes full of air spaces and decreases in volume as the water drives the air out. Rootstocks of newly planted waterlilies can be left completely exposed following this sinking effect, and where the roots have had insufficient time to penetrate the compost the whole plant will come floating to the surface. Water newly planted waterlilies like pot plants prior to placing in their permanent positions. This helps to settle the compost and drives the air out. A generous layer of washed pea shingle 2–3 cm (1 in) deep should be spread over the surface of the planting medium to discourage fish from nosing in the compost in their quest for aquatic insect larvae and so clouding the water (Fig. 7b).

In a newly constructed pool the planted baskets should ideally be placed in their final positions with enough water run in to cover the crowns. As the young foliage starts to grow the water level can be slowly raised. When adding a waterlily to an established pool, then this procedure can be reversed. The basket can be stood on a pile of bricks and gradually lowered by removing the bricks one at a time one as the growths lengthen. When baskets have to be placed in a tricky position in the centre of the pool, lengths of string can be threaded through either side of the basket. Two people are then needed, one each side of the pool, to lower the basket gently into place.

Marginal plants are planted in the same manner as waterlilies, but submerged plants are treated differently.

These are usually sold as bunches of unrooted cuttings fastened together near the base with a strip of lead. Although seeming to be clinging precariously to life, once introduced to a pool they rapidly initiate roots and grow away strongly. They do not rely entirely upon nutrients supplied by the compost and can indeed exist for a considerably length of the time just floating about in the water. But rooting gives them stability. The important point to remember when planting the bunches is to bury the lead weight (Fig. 8). If exposed to the water it quickly rots through the stems and the top of the plant falls away.

Introducing floating plants could not be simpler: they are merely tossed on to the surface of the water where they live happily without coming into direct contact with soil or compost.

WATERLILIES

The waterlilies (*Nymphaea*) flower more or less continuously from early summer until the first autumn frosts. The letters in parentheses indicate the vigour of the variety and its most suitable depth of water. All the following varieties are frost hardy. S = small: 15–30 cm (6 in–1 ft), M = medium; 30–60 cm (1–2 ft) L = large; 60–90 cm (2–3 ft).

'Amabilis'
Large, pointed salmon pink flowers which age to soft rose. Yellow centres intensify to fiery orange. Large, deep green leaves. (M)

'Charles de Meurville'
A strong-growing plant with large plum coloured blossoms tipped and streaked with white. Olive green foliage. (L)

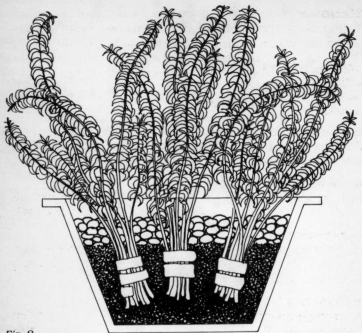

Fig. 8
Submerged oxygenating plants are usually sold as bunches of
unrooted cuttings, fastened together at the base with a strip of
lead, which acts as a weight to hold them down.

'Froebeli'
Deep blood red flowers with orange centres. Dull
purplish leaves. Free-flowering. (M)

'Gonnère'
Double, pure white globular flowers. Luxuriant pea
green leaves. Sometimes sold under the name 'Crystal
White'. (L)

'Graziella'
Orange-red flowers which age to red. Olive green leaves
blotched with purple and brown. (M)

'Hermine'
Tulip-shaped flowers of pure white are held slightly above the water. Dark green oval leaves. (L)

'James Brydon'
Large crimson, paeony-shaped blossoms float among dark purplish green leaves which are often flecked with maroon. (L)

laydekeri **'Fulgens'**
Fragrant bright crimson flowers with reddish centres. Dark green leaves with purplish undersides. (M)

laydekeri **'Purpurata'**
Rich vinous red blooms borne in profusion among small dark green leaves with purplish undersides. (M)

marliacea **'Albida'**
Large white fragrant blossoms with golden centres. The backs of the petals are often flushed with soft pink. Deep green leaves with purplish undersides. (L)

marliacea **'Carnea'**
A strong-growing flesh pink variety which is also called 'Morning Glory'. Flowers on newly established plants are often white for the first few months. Vanilla scented. (L)

marliacea **'Chromatella'**
An old and popular variety. Large soft yellow flowers are produced among handsome mottled foliage. (L)

'Mrs Richmond'
Beautiful pale rose pink flowers which pass to crimson with age. Plain green leaves. (L)

odorata **'Firecrest'**
Deep pink flowers and striking purplish green leaves. (L)

odorata minor
A splendid miniature variety with fragrant star-shaped

flowers and soft green leaves. Ideal for tubs, sinks and very shallow pools. (S)

odorata 'Sulphurea'

A popular canary yellow variety with dark green, heavily mottled foliage. Flowers star-shaped and slightly fragrant. (M)

pygmaea 'Alba'

The tiniest white variety available. Small dark green leaves. (S)

pygmaea 'Helvola'

Beautiful canary yellow flowers with orange centres are produced continuously throughout the summer. Olive green foliage heavily mottled with purple and brown. (S)

'René Gérard'

Broad open flowers with narrow rose pink petals blotched and splashed with crimson towards the centre. Plain green leaves. (L)

'Rose Arey'

Large open star-like flowers with bright golden centres and an overpowering aniseed fragrance. (L)

'William Falconer'

Medium-sized upright bright red flowers with yellow centres. Foliage purplish when young, but turning olive green with age. (L)

DEEP-WATER AQUATICS

In addition to the waterlilies there are a couple of other aquatics, also frost hardy, which prosper in deep water and are worth considering. The figures given are the depths at which each will grow best.

Aponogeton distachyus Water Hawthorn
Small floating dark green leaves and pure white vanilla-scented blossoms that are produced for much of the summer. 30–90 cm (1–3 ft).

Nymphoides peltata Water Fringe
Delicately fringed buttercup-like flowers and small waterlily-like leaves. Summer. 30–75 cm (1–2½ ft).

MARGINAL PLANTS

It is the marginal plants that occupy the shallow shelves around the edge of the pool. These will grow happily in several centimetres of water or just wet conditions. The figures given are the heights usually attained by the plants under good growing conditions. All are frost hardy.

Acorus calamus 'Variegatus'
Cream and green iris-like foliage flushed with pink in early spring. 30–60 cm (1–2 ft).

Alisma plantago-aquatica Water Plantain
Narrow oval foliage and symmetrical spikes of white flowers flushed with pink. Summer. 45–75 cm (1½–2½ ft).

Butomus umbellatus Flowering Rush
Twisted green rush-like foliage surmounted by large heads of rose pink flowers. Late summer. 45–75 cm (1½–2½ ft).

Calla palustris Bog Arum
A member of the arum lily family, with white sail-like flowers followed by red fruits. Spring. 30 cm (1 ft).

Caltha palustris Marsh Marigold
Bright yellow flowers above dark green glossy foliage.

The variety 'Flore Pleno' is shorter and fully double. Spring. 30–75 cm (1–2½ ft).

Caltha polypetala Himalayan Marsh Marigold
With glistening golden blossoms like the ordinary marsh marigold, but much larger in every part. Spring. 90 cm (3 ft).

Eriophorum angustifolium Cotton Grass
Grassy leaves and distinctive cottonwool-like seeding heads. Acid-loving. Summer. (30–60 cm (1–2 ft).

***Glyceria aquatica* 'Variegata'** Variegated Water Grass
Green and cream striped leaves with pink tints during early spring. 75–90 cm (2½–3 ft).

Iris laevigata
A splendid blue-flowered aquatic iris which has given rise to many fine varieties: 'Rose Queen' is pink, 'Alba' white, 'Monstrosa' purple and white, while 'Variegata' has handsome white and green striped foliage. Summer. 60 cm (2 ft).

***Iris pseudacorus* 'Variegatus'**
Yellow flowers and superb cream and green variegated foliage. 60–75 cm (2–2½ ft).

Mentha aquatica Water Mint
Strongly aromatic, with creeping downy foliage and whorls of pink flowers. Late summer. 30–45 cm (1–1½ ft).

Menyanthes trifoliata Bog Bean
Dark green broad bean-like leaves sprinkled with delicate white-fringed flowers. Late spring. 30 cm (1 ft).

Myosotis scorpioides Water Forget-me-not
A lovely blue-flowered perennial of similar appearance to our traditional bedding forget-me-not. Late spring and early summer. 30 cm (1 ft).

***Ranunculus lingua* 'Grandiflora'**
A strong-growing member of the buttercup family with

large bold golden blossoms. Early summer. 75–90 cm
(2½–3 ft).

Sagittaria japonica Japanese Arrowhead
Bold arrow-shaped foliage and spikes of single white
flowers. The variety 'Plena' is fully double. Summer.
60 cm (2 ft).

Scirpus 'Albescens'
Sulphurous white stems with a longditudinal green
stripe and tassels of brownish flowers. 60–90 cm (2–3 ft).

Scirpus lacustris Bulrush
Dark green pencil-thick needle-like rushes. Brownish
flowers. 60–90 cm (2–3 ft).

Scirpus tabernaemontani 'Zebrinus'
A popular rush with needle-like stems horizontally
barred with green and white. 60–90 cm (2–3 ft).

Typha minima
A completely dwarf reedmace with slender grey-green
foliage and typical hard chocolate coloured seed heads.
Late summer. 30 cm (1 ft).

Veronica beccabunga Brooklime
Evergreen scrambling foliage sprinkled with tiny starry
blue flowers. Ideal for masking the harsh edge of a pool.
Summer. 15–30 cm (6 in–1 ft).

SUBMERGED PLANTS

These are the plants popularly referred to as 'water
weeds' which inhabit the lower reaches of the pool.
They are often not particularly decorative, but they do
perform an essential role in maintaining a balance
within the pool. All will prosper in the average pool,
mostly tolerating depths of 1 m (3 ft) or more.

Apium inundatum Water Celery
Divided celery-like leaves and crowded heads of small white flowers above the surface of the water.

Callitriche platycarpa Starwort
Whorls of pea green, submerged leaves, occasional floating foliage during the summer.

Ceratophyllum demersum Hornwort
Dense whorls of dark green bristly foliage. An excellent plant for difficult cool shady places.

Elodea canadensis Canadian Pondweed
A vigorous, but excellent submerged plant. Dense bushy stems with whorls of dark green leaves.

Fontinalis antipyretica Willow Moss
A useful evergreen species for dark areas and moving water.

Hottonia palustris Water Violet
Large whorls of lime-green divided foliage support bold erect spikes of lilac or white blossoms during early summer.

Lagarosiphon major Goldfish Weed
Probably the most widely grown submerged aquatic of all. It is this dark green crispy-leaved plant that is sold in large numbers by pet shops for goldfish bowls.

Myriophyllum spicatum Spiked Milfoil
Small crimson flowers are borne on the ends of soft, feathery, grey-green foliage.

Potomogeton crispus Curled Pondweed
Handsome foliage like a bronze-green seaweed. Translucent with crinkled edges and supporting short spikes of relatively insignificant crimson and cream flowers.

Ranunculus aquatilis Water Crowfoot
Deeply dissected submerged foliage and clover-like floating leaves which give rise to tiny pure gold and white blossoms during early summer.

FLOATING PLANTS

Floating aquatics make a major contribution to the balance of the pool by providing surface shade. Along with the deep water aquatics they provide a cool haven for ornamental fish on a hot summer's day. They also effectively reduce the intensity of light beneath the water, thereby making it difficult for primitive green water-discolouring algae to become established. With the exception of *Eichhornia crassipes*, all are frost hardy.

Azolla caroliniana Fairy Moss
This little member of the fern family has coarse green floating fronds. When young or growing in shade they are green, but turn red at the approach of winter or in full sun.

Eichhornia crassipes Water Hyacinth
A tender aquatic from South America which is usually grown as an annual and placed on the pool after the danger of frost has passed. It has bold glossy leaves with inflated bulbous bases which assist with buoyancy. The flowers are lavender blue and reminiscent of a tropical orchid.

Hydrocharis morsus-ranae Frogbit
This looks rather like a small waterlily, having tiny kidney-shaped floating leaves in neat floating rosettes. The flowers are three-petalled and produced during summer.

Stratiotes aloides Water Soldier
Large spiky rosettes of bronze-green foliage very much like a pineapple top. Papery white or pinkish blossoms are produced during late summer.

Trapa natans Water Chestnut
Rosettes of dark green rhomboidal leaves support creamy white axillary flowers.

Utricularia vulgaris Bladderwort
A strange rootless floating plant with sprawling stems of feathery foliage that conceal tiny bladders which trap unwary aquatic insects. Spikes of bright yellow antirrhinum-like flowers during summer.

BOG GARDEN PLANTS

Damp areas at the poolside provide an excellent home for bog garden plants. These rarely enjoy standing in water, but benefit from really marshy conditions, preferably with plenty of organic matter incorporated. The figures given are the heights usually attained by the plants under good growing conditions.

Aruncus sylvester 'Kneiffi' Dwarf Goat's Beard
Dwarf fluffy white plumes of blossom above much divided pale green foliage. Summer. 60–90 cm (2–3 ft).

Astilbe arendsii
Formerly known as spiraeas, these have spires of frothy flowers above compact, deeply cut foliage. 'Red Sentinel', 'Perle Rose' and the dwarf white 'Irrlicht' are all good varieties. Summer. 60–90 cm (2–3 ft).

Cardamine pratensis Cuckoo Flower
A charming spring-flowering waterside plant with single lilac-rose blossoms and hummocks of pale green fern-like foliage. The double form, 'Flore Plena' is even more lovely. 30 cm (1 ft).

Filipendula ulmaria 'Aurea'
This is a golden foliage form of the lovely meadowsweet. Its flowers are best removed to improve the quantity of the foliage. 30 cm (1 ft).

Hosta fortunei
A majestic large-leaved plantain lily. Apart from its

beautifully sculptured pale green leaves it has bold spikes of handsome lilac funnel-shaped blossoms. Summer. 30–45 cm (1–1½ ft).

Hosta undulata medio-variegata
One of the most popular variegated hostas, with twisted and undulating leaves in cream, green and white. Its paltry flowers are best removed to enhance the quality of its foliage. 30 cm (1 ft).

Houttuynia cordata
Strange-smelling bluish-green heart-shaped leaves on reddish stems support curious small white conical flowers. There is a double flowered form, 'Pleno', which is more desirable. The foliage is a great asset, for it is produced on creeping stems that carpet the ground around taller growing plants. Summer. 30–45 cm (1–1½ ft).

Iris kaempferi Japanese Clematis Flowered Iris
Strong tufts of broad grassy foliage support large brightly coloured clematis-like blossoms. There are many named varieties, but the mixed Higo strain produces the most spectacular flowers. This iris must have an acid soil. Summer 60–75 cm (2–2½ ft).

Iris sibirica Siberian Iris
An easily grown iris with clumps of grassy foliage and attractive flowers. Not fussy about soil conditions and will flourish in both wet and just slightly damp conditions. There are many varieties, but 'Perry's Blue' is the best known. Summer. 60–75 cm (2–2½ ft).

Primula
There are endless primulas that can be grown under bog garden conditions. These comprise most of the late spring- and summer-flowering candelabra species and hybrids. These include the red *P. japonica* 60 cm (2 ft) and *P. pulverulenta* 75 cm (2½ ft), the orange *P. chungensis* 30 cm (1 ft) as well as the rosy purple

P. beesiana 60 cm (2 ft) and yellow *P. helodoxa* 60 cm (2 ft). Other kinds of primula that do well are the early-flowering drumstick primula, *P. denticulata*, 30–45 cm (1–1½ ft), the cowslip-like *P. florindae* 90 cm (3 ft) and the tiny ground-hugging *P. rosea* 15 cm (6 in).

Trollius europaeus Globe Flower
Buttercup-like plants with globular blossoms in shades of orange, cream and yellow. The foliage is large and dark green, similar in shape to the common buttercup. There are many named kinds, but 'Orange Crest' and 'Golden Queen' are among the best. Late spring and early summer. 75 cm (2½ ft).

RAISING A FEW PLANTS

Most pool owners like to raise a few plants, if only to give away to friends. Just because aquatic plants live in water, it does not mean to say that they are any more difficult to increase than their land-dwelling cousins. Special conditions are not required, most young water plants being capable of being raised in a large household bowl on the kitchen window ledge.

WATERLILIES

It is relatively simple to raise waterlilies from 'eyes', even though it takes two or more years to produce a flowering-size crown. The eyes are really latent growing points which occur with varying frequency along the scrambling rootstock of adult plants. If these are removed at the time when the mature plant is being divided or replanted, they can be rooted and grown into independent plants. The ideal period is during late spring or early summer, although propagation can continue until late summer. Most eyes have to be removed with a knife, although some can be detached by hand. Raw surfaces should be dressed with sulphur or charcoal to prevent fungal infection and the severed eyes potted individually in good clean garden soil and stood in a bowl of water on the window ledge. The adult plant can be returned to the pool. As the emerging leaf stalks lengthen on the new plantlets, the water level in the bowl should be raised. The plants must then be potted progressively until large enough to be capable of surviving in a proper aquatic planting basket.

A few of the miniature waterlilies, like the ever-popular *Nymphaea pygmaea* 'Alba', have to be increased from seed. Seed must be fresh and have been kept moist to be successful; dried seed is most unlikely to germinate. Freshly harvested seed is mixed in with a thick jelly-like substance from which it is virtually impossible to remove the individual seeds. In order to avoid damage, therefore, it is advisable to sow the seeds with the jelly. A good clean garden soil, as recommended for eyes, should be used, the water level in the bowl just covering the surface of the compost. The first seedlings will appear after a couple of weeks and look like small translucent liverworts. At this time they are vulnerable to damage by filamentous algae which should be controlled by the regular use of an algaecide. Once the seedlings are producing floating foliage they are large enough to be pricked out into trays in the usual manner, eventually being transferred to individual pots.

OTHER METHODS OF PROPAGATION

Most other aquatic plants can be dealt with in a similar way to waterlilies, although a number, like *Pontederia cordata* and *Aponogeton distachyus*, should not be allowed to dry out and must be sown fresh. Others, such as *Myosotis scorpioides* and *Alisma plantago-aquatica* can be stored for a while and will still germinate satisfactorily.

Creeping aquatics, like *Veronica beccabunga* and *Menyanthes trifoliata*, are easily grown from short stem cuttings taken at any time during the growing season. These should be about 5 cm (2 in) long and inserted in a tray of mud. Rooting takes place quickly and the young plants can be potted individually.

The majority of the reeds and rushes, together with aquatic irises and marsh marigolds, are increased by division. This needs doing periodically anyway, mature plants being carefully lifted and divided in the same way as ordinary herbaceous perennials. Two small hand forks placed back to back in the centre of a clump and then prised apart is the way to separate tough plants. Always select healthy young outer shoots for propagation and replanting, discarding the central portion if old and tough.

CHAPTER 5

FISH AND OTHER LIVESTOCK

As soon as the pool has been planted there is always a great temptation to introduce the fish. This urge should be resisted for at least four or five weks so that the plants can become established. If fish are put into a freshly planted pool they root among the plants, disturbing them and retarding their growth. Even a generous layer of pea shingle covering the surface of the container will not prevent this from happening.

STOCKING WITH FISH

The most satisfactory stocking rate for ornamental fish is 5 cm of length of fish to every 0.1 square metre or 2 in of fish for every square foot of surface area. This is not of the total surface area of the pool, but of open water uncluttered by marginal plants. This rate of stocking permits growth and development of the fish and makes natural breeding quite likely. The calculation of the length of fish in this formula is based upon the total length from nose to tail Therefore, if a total length of 90 cm (3 ft) is calculated as the ideal, the fish population could consist of three fish each 30 cm (1 ft) long, six fish 15 cm (6 in) long or any combination of each that results in a total length of 90 cm (3 ft).

SELECTING ORNAMENTAL FISH

A well-balanced mixture of healthy ornamental fish is vital if the pool is to be a success. Most of those which are sold in Northern Europe and North America are imported from warmer climates where they breed more freely. This does not mean that they are any more vulnerable to cooler weather, for all those commonly sold adapt readily.

A good guide as to whether a fish is in satisfactory health is the condition of its fins. Stout or well expanded fins indicate good health and this can be confirmed if the eyes are clear and bright as well. Also, choose only lively fish.

With small fish it is important to see that there are no damaged or missing scales, as exposed tissue is very susceptible to fungal infection. The same applies to larger specimens, although it is not quite so critical, and the likelihood of finding a large fish that has no scales missing is fairly remote. If an otherwise healthy fish has a few scales missing, then dip it in one of the proprietary fungus cures. It is prudent in any event to treat all newly purchased fish in this way, giving them a dousing with a solution of either malachite green or methylene blue as a precaution before introducing them to the pond.

When decorative pond fish are purchased they are usually packed in heavy-gauge polythene bags which are blown up with oxygen. Fish travel quite happily this way in normal circumstances, but it is advisable to ensure that large specimens are packed individually. If the weather is hot or thundery resist the temptation of buying fish such as golden orfe which have a high oxygen requirement, for the chances are that they will succumb on the way home.

Freshly purchased fish should be introduced to the

pool gradually. If the bag has been blown up with oxygen allow it to float on the surface of the pool for a short time so that the temperature of the water inside becomes equalized with that in the pool, and then gently pour the fish out.

All the ornamental coldwater fish described here will live happily together. Even young fish, once they are past the fry stage, will mix quite successfully with all sizes and both sexes of the varieties listed. Fish of all kinds grow in accordance with their surroundings, thus a goldfish that has been confined to a bowl for a number of years will remain small, yet once introduced to a pool will increase in size quickly.

Goldfish

There can be few people who are not familiar with the common goldfish. In its various shades of reds, pinks, yellows and orange it is probably the best known and most popular garden pool fish of all.

Apart from obvious differences in colour, the most striking divergence from the true goldfish is the transparent scaled variety, the shubunkin. In this, the body appears smooth and scaleless and in all manner of colour combinations. Reds, yellows, blues and violets intermingle and are often splashed and stained with crimson or black.

Apart from the wide and variable colour range exhibited by both goldfish and shubunkins, there are actual strains, particularly within the shubunkins, which are very fine and breed true to character. Two of these are especially nice and worthy of special mention and the highest possible recommendation. The first is the Cambridge Blue Shubunkin, a fish with an even base of powder blue overlaid with violet and occasional patches of ochre, although these latter in the eyes of the connoisseur are undesirable. The other is the Bristol Blue Shubunkin, a strain developed by a group of enthusiasts in Bristol in which the base colour is again blue but heavily overlaid with violet and mauve and liberally splashed with crimson.

Varieties of the preceding are available in comet longtail form. These are fish in which the tails are long and flowing, often as long as the body and give the appearance of a comet. In the blue forms of shubunkins they are exceptionally fine and comparable with the most exotic tropical fish.

Fantails and moors are varieties of goldfish with short dumpy bodies and tripartite tails. The fantails have characteristic goldfish heads, while the moors have somewhat bulbous telescopic eyes. Both forms occur in goldfish and shubunkins. The goldfish types of fantail are known as red or red and white fantails and the shubunkin types as calico fantails. Moors fall into similar popular classes; the shubunkins being known as calico moors, red goldfish types as red telescopes and the well-known black variety as black moors. The latter are exceptionally beautiful fish and worthy of special praise, their bodies being of the most intense and gorgeous velvety black.

Twin-tailed goldfish of the same general appearances as fantails and moors but with long drooping extended tails are generally known as veiltails. Apart from possessing an extraordinarily long and fine pendant tail, the oranda has a curious strawberry-like growth on the head. Otherwise it is identical to the typical veiltail. A further, and what one might consider final, departure from this is the lionhead; a fish with similar strawberry-like excrescences on its head which call to mind a lion's mane and a short chubby body that is entirely devoid of a dorsal fin. However, there is one more variety that exceeds all others with its bizarre appearance and that is the one known as the celestial. Its body is fairly typical of the conventional goldfish, but with a head that is flattened and bears two upward looking eyes.

All goldfish and shubunkins are hardy in their natural forms, but many of the fancy kinds will not tolerate being frozen in the ice and unless a minimum depth of 45 cm (18 in) can be provided at least at one point in the pool, then they are best avoided. If you have more interest in the plants than the fish, or through force of circumstances can spend only a little time with your pond then you should leave fancy goldfish alone, for with their slow and ungainly manner of movement they are easy prey for all manner of diseases and natural predators. However, for the fortunate pool owner with ample time to observe his fish and pander to their slightest whim, few can be so rewarding as the fancy varieties of goldfish.

Carp

The majority of fish encountered in the garden pool are members of the carp family. Common goldfish and shubunkins are derived from a species of carp. Those referred to by pool owners as carp include many undesirable coarse fish which are uninteresting in appearance and boisterous in the small pool. The only two kinds to consider are the Chinese red carp or Higoi and the Japanese Nishiki-Koi or Koi carp. The Higoi is a meaty salmon-pink coloured fish with a blunt head and pendant barbels, while the Koi is of similar shape and appearance but with brightly coloured scales that often have a metallic lustre.

Orfe

There are both golden and silver orfe, but it is only the golden variety which is widely available. This is a sleek surface-swimming fish of an orange-pink colour which when mature looks like a well-proportioned carrot swimming in the water. Orfe are shoal fish which should be introduced in threes or fours as a minimum.

SCAVENGING FISH, SNAILS AND MUSSELS

There is a common misconception among pool owners that garden pools will not function successfully without scavenging fish and snails. This has been brought about because many pool owners believe that scavengers are living vacuum cleaners and will suck up and eat mud, debris, stones and all the undesirable accumulation of the pool floor. What they actually do is to devour uneaten goldfish food, which if left to accumulate on the bottom of the pool would grow fungus and pollute the water. Snails feed to a limited extent upon such detritus, but are included in a pool to eat algae, particularly the filamentous kind that clings to submerged oxygenating plants and aquatic planting baskets.

Tench

The most popular scavenging fish is the tench, a refined and dignified character. Unseen once placed in the pool, tench are handsome sleek grey-green fish with smooth slimy bodies.

Freshwater snails

There are many different aquatic snails that can be introduced to the garden pool, but only the ramshorn snail can be relied upon to confine its activities to grazing on algae. The common freshwater whelk or greater pond snail which is frequently offered for sale by garden centres will eat algae, but is equally partial to waterlily foliage.

The ramshorn snail is a distinctive character, with a rounded flat shell like a Catherine wheel which the creature carries in an upright fashion on its back. The body is usually black, but sometimes red or white. The freshwater whelk, on the other hand, has a tall, spiralled shell and a greyish body. Both are often introduced to the pool unwittingly as eggs on the foliage of aquatic plant. The eggs of the desirable ramshorn kind are produced in a flat pad of jelly which is often seen stuck beneath the floating foliage of deep-water aquatics and waterlilies. The eggs of the freshwater whelk are produced in a small cigar-shaped cylinder of jelly which may be attached to any part of a plant. The removal of the latter at planting time will prevent a lot of problems later.

Freshwater Mussels

There are two kinds of freshwater mussel generally available from water garden specialists. Both are equally useful in an established pool when there is an accumulation of debris on the pool floor where they can live in peace. The swan mussel has a brownish green shell with a white fleshy body, while the painter's mussel has a yellowish shell with distinctive brown markings. Both draw in algae-laden water, retain the algae and discharge clear water.

Frogs

These splendid creatures are naturally occurring additions to pool life, feeding on harmful insect pests, producing tadpoles and splashing around in an eccentric manner. Beloved of small boys, these lumbering amphibians rarely cause any problem. The bad reputation which some people give them has been derived from occasional reports of male frogs clasping on to adult fish in a mating embrace and causing damage to the unfortunate host. These occurrences are rare and only happen in pools where there are no female frogs.

Toads

Great friends of the gardener because of their preferred diet of slugs and other garden pests, toads are not so frequently seen in the pool, although their spawn is often deposited there. Every encouragement should be given to retain these characters and a stone or two placed in the vicinity beneath which they can hide is a good idea.

Newts

Confused with lizards by many people, these insectivorous amphibians are common visitors to the garden pool. The common newt is a brownish or olive colour, the male being enhanced by a rippling crest along its back and a reddish or orange belly. Common newts only live in the water for a short period of time, when carrying out their courtship and depositing eggs. For the remainder of the year they rest beneath stones during the heat of the day and become torpid and more or less hibernate during the winter. Great crested newts, on the other hand, live for most of the year in the water where they breed successfully. Lovely black lizard-like amphibians with brilliant yellow bellies, the very survival of this protected species depends upon us giving them sanctuary in our garden pools.

BREEDING A FEW FISH

It is fun and instructive to try breeding a few fish, even if they eventually have to be given away to friends. However, for some pool owners fish breeding has its serious side and in many cases the garden pool is not planted so much for the benefit of the human eye as for the well-being and proliferation of the fish. All the fish that are commonly sold for pools will belong to the carp family. Therefore they all have similar requirements for their successful reproduction, although certain species, notably orfe and tench, sometimes seem loath to breed freely in captivity. All the species known collectively as carp, and of course the common goldfish and its forms, reproduce freely and many interbreed with one another.

The breeding season lasts from late spring until late summer, the sexual urges of the fish being stimulated by the warmth and light intensity associated with these seasons. Most goldfish are sexually mature in their second year, although adulthood is related more directly to size than age. Any goldfish 8 cm (3 in) or more in length should be capable of reproduction. Many people start breeding fish by purchasing one or two matched pairs of goldfish, and while this is to be recommended, it does not follow that the pair purchased will breed with each other if there are other sizeable fish in the pond. Generally like breed with like, but hybrids in the carp family are common and those of similar shape and constitution do interbreed. Sexing fish in the spring is fairly easy. Body shape when looked at from above is oval or elliptical for the female, and slim and pencil-like for the male. Differentiation is further enhanced by the male's white pimple-like nuptial tubercles which are sprinkled liberally over his gill plates and often on top of his head as well.

Spawnings take place at any time during the breeding season, several occurring each year, but their frequency is unpredictable and seems to be linked with water temperature and similar factors. During spawning the male fish chases the female around the pool and among the submerged plants, brushing and pushing furiously against her flanks. The female then releases the spawn, trailing it among the stems and foliage of submerged plant life. The male then releases his milt or sperm-bearing fluid among the eggs which then become fertilized. When this has happened the adults should if possible be separated from the area in which the spawn has been deposited, otherwise the spawn is liable to be eaten! Alternatively, plants covered in spawn can be removed to an aquarium containing pond water. The use of the same water is most important as it will be of the same temperature and chemical composition as that in the pool and consequently not injurious to the eggs.

Within three or four days the fry will be seen to be developing. First of all they are difficult to see, resembling tiny pins in the water clinging to submerged plants. After a couple of weeks they are recognizable as fish, sometimes transparent, occasionally bronze, but all eventually attaining their correct adult proportions. Often fish will remain bronze until quite large, sometimes not changing to the rich oranges, reds and yellows which are normally associated with goldfish. This delay in colour change is associated with water temperature. The lower the temperature at spawning the longer it will take for them to change colour. Irrespective of the pool owner's attention, if there are goldfish and carp in the pool and the sexes are reasonably evenly balanced breeding will take place and a handful of young fish will almost certainly be successfully raised.

CHAPTER 6

POOL MAINTENANCE

The garden pool is easy to care for, but each year there are some jobs that will need to be carried out if it is to look its best. Compared with many other parts of the garden the pool is relatively maintenance-free.

CARING FOR THE POOL IN SPRING

Although it is often suggested that a pool should be cleaned out in spring, this need not be an annual task. A pool that is disturbed too often is unlikely to return to a nice healthy balance with clear water until well into the summer. It is only necessary to clean the pool out completely when there is a substantial accumulation of organic debris on the pool floor and difficulty in keeping the water absolutely clear. An oily scum may appear on the surface of the water, sometimes accompanied by an unpleasant smell. A thorough spring clean should only be necessary every five or six years; otherwise it is merely a case of lifting and dividing overgrown plants and replanting them in fresh compost.

Before spring cleaning can begin, the pool must be drained. If you have an established concrete pool it may have a drainage plug, but it is more usual to have to resort to siphoning or bailing the water out. Siphoning presents no problem if some of the surrounding ground is lower than the pool. A length of hosepipe is filled with water and, while one end is submerged in the pool with the thumb over it, the other end is removed to a lower area. As long as this is done in sequence and the end of the hosepipe outside the pool is lower that that in the pool, gravity will withdraw the water.

If the pool has been constructed in the lowest part of the garden, then the water will have to be bailed out with a bucket. Great care should be taken to ensure than fish and snails are not thrown out with the water. Most fish will linger in the mud and debris on the pool floor and can then be easily caught. When emptying the pool it is a good idea to have one or two buckets of water nearby in order to provide instant accommodation for rescued fish.

Fish that have been removed should be placed in as cool a place as possible while spring cleaning takes place. A garage or outhouse are ideal, the fish being put in bowls or buckets of pool water with as large a surface area as possible. Snails should be kept separately in a jar, as when they are put with fish in a confined space they are likely to be sucked out of their shells and eaten.

Fish that are swimming around in a bucket will have little natural food to eat, even if generous quantities of pondweed are put in with them, so a pinch of fish food every day is vital.

Aquatic plants also need careful attention, especially the submerged aquatics. These dry out very quickly if exposed to the air. Put some of the best pieces in buckets of water in a cool but light place. When ready for replanting these can be bunched up as cuttings and fastened togther with a lead weight or a short piece of wire. Waterlilies will last for some days just wrapped up in polythene, while marginal plants are likely to be happy for a week or so if kept in a cool light place where their roots will not dry out.

Such an upheaval need only take place occasionally. Usually there are replacements to be made for the occasional plant losses of winter, and of course some plants will need lifting and dividing if they are to retain their vigour. As a rule marginal plants should be lifted and divided every two or three years, but it is undesirable to lift large numbers of plants at one time as when replanted the pool will look sparsely furnished for a while. A policy of lifting certain groups of plants each year is the most sensible and ensures an acceptable appearance throughout.

Waterlilies do not need attention so often. The third year after planting is the most appropriate time to divide vigorous kinds, while some of the more restrained varieties will last for four or five years without attention. The need for division is apparent when the plants make a preponderance of small leafy growth in the centre of the clump, often accompanied by diminishing flower size.

Submerged plants can often be left for a number of years without attention, although the stringy winter growth of semi-evergreen kinds like the curled pondweed should be cut off each spring to allow fresh growth to break from the base. When a basket of submerged plants is not prospering it is a good idea to shake out the soil and replant healthy young cuttings in fresh compost.

To divide marginal plants, separate the rootstocks by inserting two hand forks back to back and then levering them apart. Always replant pieces of plant from the other edge of the clump as this is young, vigorous and more readily established. Waterlilies can be treated similarly, except that in most cases they will need to be separated with a knife. Care should be taken to see that any open wounds are dressed with powdered charcoal to prevent infection. The rootstock of a healthy mature waterlily consists of a main fleshy root, which was the one originally planted, together with a number of side branches. It is these side growths that should be kept, the original rootstock being discarded. Each severed branch will produce a plant, providing that it has a healthy terminal shoot.

LOOKING AFTER THE POOL IN SUMMER

During the summer the pool largely takes care of itself. Dead flower heads should be regularly removed to prevent plants from exhausting themselves by setting seed. This also prevents the haphazard distribution of seed around the pool.

FEEDING PLANTS AND FISH

Most plants that have not been repotted in fresh compost benefit from some fertilizer. Modern aquatic plant fertilizers are available in perforated sachets and these are pushed into the compost next to the plants and release plant nutrients at the roots rather than into the water where an increased level of plant foods would encourage the rapid development of algae. This form of fertilizing aquatic plants is excellent, but somewhat more expensive than using traditional bonemeal 'pills'. These are made from coarse bonemeal rolled into balls of clay. Each serves in a similar way to a sachet of fertilizer, a ball being pushed into the compost of each planting basket close by plants that have remained undisturbed.

Although it is not vital, most pool owners like to feed their fish regularly. In most pools it is unnecessary as there are always sufficient aquatic insects around to satisfy the most voracious appetites. However, much of the enjoyment of owning a pool is in feeding the fish. Regular feeding at the same place in the pool encourages the fish to become tame and appear at that spot at the sound of a footfall or the casting of a shadow. Feeding fish can be likened in many ways to feeding plants, for not all varieties have the same requirements. Overfeeding can be both wasteful, and in a small pool dangerous, as any uneaten food is likely to decompose and pollute the water.

Balanced fish foods are available in three different forms. The conventional crumb food is usually in a mixture of colours from white and ochre to red and vivid yellow. This is often the by-product of biscuit manufacture. The flaked foods are also multi-coloured, but take the form of thin tissues of flake rather like a much refined breakfast cereal. Then there are the floating pellet varieties which are of even size and a brownish colour. All have their advocates and each their drawbacks. Both pelleted and flaked foods float for a considerable length of time. This is an obvious benefit, but on windy days the flakes may be carried on the breeze and end up out of the reach of the fish in the tangle of plants at the poolside. It does not matter too much which food is used, or even if a combination of diet is arranged, for fish adapt readily to a change of diet, and will continue to thrive.

During the summer months feeding the equivalent of a pinch of food for each fish on alternate days is adequate. Pay attention to the speed at which the fish clear up the food. Any that remains floating around after twenty minutes should be netted off and the rate of feeding reduced until a happy balance is achieved.

ALGAE CONTROL

Algae control is a summer occupation. Even in the best maintained and balanced pool algae of one kind or another will appear. Although a nuisance it is not a sign of an unhealthy pool, rather is it an indication of a nutrient-rich one. Algae are tiny, primitive plants which occur in a wide range of forms, from the free-floating dust-like kinds to the clinging mermaid's hair and the long filamentous spirogyra. The tiniest sorts are suspended in the water and if you pass your hand through, a greenish smear is deposited. Filamentous algae are more substantial and can be pulled out of the water by the handful, while the kind known as mermaid's hair clings to baskets and the poolside and can be removed in tufts if pulled sharply.

Control of the free-floating kinds is not difficult with an algaecide based upon potassium permanganate, but its effect is short-lived and if not carefully administered during warm weather will turn the water yellow. Filamentous algae can be controlled with algaecides based upon copper sulphate, but it is important that all dead algae are removed after treatment to prevent the de-oxygenation of the water. Proprietary algaecides should always be used: never experiment with chemicals.

These algal controls are not permanent cures for the problem, nor do they replace the natural balance which produces long-term, sweet, mellow water and healthy conditions. They are essentially temporary aids for a new pool until the submerged plants have become established and can compete on an equal footing with the algae. They can also be used in difficult periods in an established pool, particularly during early summer when an algal bloom may develop before the pool plants have really got growing.

PREPARING FOR WINTER

It is important not to forget the pool during the autumn and winter months. If neglected, problems can occur with fallen leaves from surrounding trees. Even a small accumulation in the bottom of the pool can be dangerous, particularly if, like horse chestnut, they are toxic as well. A fine mesh net placed across the pool is absolutely essential until the trees are bare. Marginal aquatics must be cleaned up as soon as the frost has turned the foliage brown. Cut them back to about two thirds of their height. Never cut them below water level, for some aquatics have hollow stems and rot off if completely submerged. It is important, though, that all waterside plants are properly tidied up so that they do not become a winter refuge for insect pests like waterlily beetle.

Waterlilies need no winter preparation as they are perfectly hardy and die down naturally without any problem. Only the pygmy kinds, when grown in a rock pool or sink, are at risk of being damaged by severe weather. The best method of protection for these is to drain the water away and then give the rootstocks a generous covering of straw, protected by a frame light. They overwinter well like this and can easily be started into growth again in the spring by removing the straw and the covering and adding water. Floating plants disappear as the days shorten, retreating into winter buds which fall to the pool floor where they remain until the spring sunshine warms the water again.

It is useful to collect some of the overwintering buds and keep them in jars of water with a little soil in the bottom. If stood in a light frost-free place they start into growth much sooner in the spring and are an invaluable aid in the battle against algae. By being well advanced they provide surface shade a good few weeks before those that are resting naturally on the pool floor reappear.

Fish should not be neglected in the run up to winter. Feed daphnia, ants' eggs and other specialist delicacies on days when the weather is warm and bright and the fish are seen to be active. Precautions for their winter welfare should be taken at the same time, with the introduction of a pool heater or other means of keeping an ice-free area in the water. A pool heater consists of a heated brass rod with a polystyrene float which can be connected to the electrical supply which operates the pump. Even in severe weather this creates a small ice-free area, and prevents the build up of noxious gases. In a well-maintained pool the problem of gases is not so acute as there is much less organic debris to decay, but once a layer of ice has formed there is no way of knowing exactly what is going on beneath and it is a wise precaution to keep at least a small area free from ice or else fish may suffocate.

If electricity is not close at hand and the installation of an electric pool heater is impossible, the safest way of obtaining a similar effect is by standing a pan of boiling water on the ice and allowing it to melt through. Never strike the ice with a heavy instrument as this will concuss and often kill the fish.

Not only are the fish vulnerable to the effects of severe weather, but so too is the pool itself, particularly if it is made of concrete. The pressure ice can exert against the walls is often sufficient to cause cracks to appear. To overcome this, float a child's rubber ball, or even a sizeable piece of wood on the water. These are capable of expanding and contracting with the pressure of the ice and should prevent damage occuring.

PESTS AND PROBLEMS

As with all other garden features the pool is not without its share of problems. However, there are few of these that cannot be overcome by good hygiene and routine maintenance. Fortunately, few pests and diseases of plants need cause any great anxiety, although it must be appreciated that even mild infestations create difficulties beyond those encountered in the ordinary garden.

Insecticides and fungicides cannot be used in or around the pool where fish are present and so more traditional, manual means of control have to be resorted to.

Waterlily aphis　The most common and troublesome pest of aquatic plants is the waterlily aphis. It attacks leaves and flowers with impunity, having the same effect upon aquatic plants that black bean aphis have upon broad beans.

During the summer the only effective control is to spray the foliage forcibly with clear water from a hosepipe and hope that the fish will clear up the pests as they fall in the pool and before they have an opportunity to crawl back on to the foliage. Much can be done to reduce the overwintering population by spraying all the plum and cherry trees in the garden with tar oil wash during the winter months when the trees are completely dormant. This effectively breaks the life cycle.

Caddis fly larvae　Most species of caddis fly have larvae which feed to some extent upon the foliage of aquatic plants. Many are totally aquatic at their larval stage and swim around with little shelters made from sticks, sand shells and pieces of plant surrounding them. They visit the pool in the cool of the evening, depositing their eggs in a mass of jelly which swells up immediately it touches the water. Often it will be hooked around submerged foliage in a long cylindrical string, or attached to a marginal plant so that it can trail in the water.

The larvae hatch out after ten days or so, immediately starting to spin their silken cases and collecting debris and plant material with which to construct their shelters. At this time they feed voraciously upon aquatic plants, devouring leaves, stems, flowers or roots with equal indifference. They eventually pupate in the pool or among the rushes at the water's edge, emerging as dull coloured moth-like insects with greyish or brown wings. Chemical control is impossible, as the pests hide themselves in their protective shelters, but an adequate stock of fish will keep the population under control.

Waterlily beetles   Waterlily beetle is a very irritating pest to deal with. Waterlily leaves become stripped of their surface layer by the shiny black larvae and then begin to rot. The tiny dark brown beetles hibernate during the winter in poolside vegetation and migrate to the waterlilies during the early summer. Here they deposit eggs in clusters on the leaf surfaces and a week or so later hatch out into curious little black larvae with yellow bellies.

These feed on the waterlily foliage until pupation occurs, either on the leaves or surrounding aquatic plants. Under favourable conditions as many as four broods can be produced in a season. Spraying forcibly with a jet of clear water to dislodge the pests is the only remedy, although the removal of the tops of marginal plants during the early autumn will do much to prevent the adults from hiding in the vicinity of the pond and hopefully dissuade them from launching such a vigorous attack the next season.

China mark moths   The brown China mark moth is a not infrequent visitor to the garden pool, its larvae cutting and shredding the foliage from aquatic plants and providing a shelter for itself prior to pupation by sticking down pieces of leaf in which it weaves a greyish silky cocoon. The damage to plants can be extensive, chewed and distorted leaves crumbling towards the edges and surrounded by pieces of floating, decaying foliage. The eggs of these destructive caterpillars are laid during summer in neat rows along the floating foliage of aquatic plants. Within a couple of weeks the tiny caterpillars emerge and burrow into the undersides of the succulent foliage and later make small oval cases out of these leaves.

They continue to feed in this manner until the winter, hibernating for the winter period but reappearing in spring to continue their trail of destruction and weave protective cocoons prior to pupation. Small infestations can be hand picked and all pieces of innocent looking floating leaf should be netted and discarded as they may have cocoons attached. When damage is widespread it is sensible to defoliate all aquatic plants with floating leaves and consign the debris to the bonfire. All the plant species likely to be affected will rapidly regenerate healthy growth.

The beautiful China mark moth is less common, but sometimes seen. The only difference is that the caterpillars of this moth burrow into the stems of aquatic plants in the early stages of their life and eventually hibernate there, later emerging to make leaf cases and ultimately their white, silky cocoons. The only control at present is hand picking.

Waterlily leaf spot Relatively few diseases are ever encountered among aquatic plants, but waterlily leaf spot is not uncommon. This appears as dark patches on the leaves of waterlilies, eventually rotting through and causing their disintegration. It is particularly prevalent in damp humid weather. As soon as noticed, affected leaves should be removed and destroyed. A similar, but different species causes the foliage to become brown and dry at the edges, eventually crumbling and wasting away. Removal and destruction of all diseased leaves is the only effective cure.

Waterlily root rot The root rot common to waterlilies is believed to be caused by a relative of potato blight. Waterlilies with dark or mottled foliage, especially yellow-flowered varieties, seem to be the most susceptible. The leaf and flower stems become soft and blackened and the roots take on a gelatinous appearance and are foul smelling. Affected plants must be removed immediately and destroyed before they infect their neighbours. When other waterlilies are in danger of becoming infected and it is possible to remove the fish, impregnating the water with copper sulphate provides some protection. The crystals should be tied in a muslin bag attached to a long stick and dragged through the water until completely dissolved. In recent years a very virulent form of this disease has become estabilished in commercial stocks of waterlilies. This does not respond to treatment and infected plants should always be destroyed and the pool sterilized.

Fish diseases Fish are rarely troubled by pests and diseases in a well-cared-for pool, although **fin** and **tail rot** are not uncommon. This disease usually attacks the dorsal fin and then rapidly spreads to others, reducing them to short stubs. The first sign of the disease is a whitish line along the outer edge of the fin, which gradually advances downwards. This leaves the outer margin badly frayed owing to the disintegration of the soft tissue between the hard rays of the fins. If infection creeps as far as the flesh, the fish will almost certainly die. However, if an affected fish is noticed in time, the badly frayed tissue can be removed with a pair of sharp scissors and the fish dipped in malachite green. The infection is likely to be checked with this treatment and much of the lost tissue will regenerate.

Fungus is another disease which is not infrequently encountered. Every time a fish damages itself in any way it becomes open to attack from one of many fungal diseases. Apart from attacking living fish, some of these can be seen on fish spawn and uneaten goldfish food. This indicates the potential value of scavenging fish and the importance of pool hygiene. When a large fish becomes infected with fungus it is a relatively simple matter to clear it up. However, with fry and small fish it is almost impossible and any tiny fish that become infected should be humanely destroyed as soon as the disease is noticed. There are many fungus cures available, most of which are used as dips into which diseased fish are immersed. A salt bath is often recommended, and while this can be beneficial, it is a slow and unreliable method of treating this ailment. If salt must be used ensure that it is rock or sea salt, not iodized table salt. When the fish has been dipped in a proprietary fungus cure, the cottonwool-like growth of the fungus should fall away. After the fish has been re-introduced to the pool keep an eye open for re-infection as the raw areas of tissue will still be vulnerable.

Another not infrequent ailment is **white spot disease**. This is caused by a parasitic protozoon, a tiny creature which causes extensive damage to fish by becoming embedded in the skin for at least part of its life cycle. Dozens of parasites will attack a single fish, which then looks as if it has severe white measles. After a while infested fish take on a pinched, starved appearance and eventually die. Severe attacks are rarely curable and badly infested fish should be destroyed. However, mild attacks can be cured by isolating infested fish in a solution of a proprietary white spot cure based upon either acriflavine or quinine salts. Always take great care in the selection of new fish for the pool as these are often the source of infection.

DIRTY WATER

It terms of a garden pool, dirty water is not green water, but that which is brown, black, or dark blue and often has a foul smell. Brown water is the result of fish stirring up the compost in plant containers while foraging for food. If the plant containers have all been given a generous covering of pea gravel, there is rarely a problem. Sometimes if the soil is rather light it drifts out through the lattice-work sides of the container. This can be prevented by lining the container initially with a square of hessian, thus retaining the soil, but allowing water to percolate through and roots to escape. If plants have been put into containers without a generous top dressing of gravel, then the only course of action is to clean the pool out and replant.

Water that is blue-black or produces a thick whitish scum or oily film around the edges of the pool, is usually polluted by decaying organic matter, often the build-up of decomposing leaves from nearby trees. It almost inevitably has a foul smell, is very low in oxygen and regular deaths of fish and snails occur. A thorough clean out is the only answer. The walls of the pool must be well scrubbed and it is advantageous if the pool can then be left to dry out in the open air for a day or two. Any plants that look in good health can be returned to the pool, but not without being thoroughly washed and replanted in good clean compost in containers that have received a vigorous scrubbing.

DEALING WITH A HERON

Apart from all the problems that may occur within the pool, there is one that may quite unexpectedly come from outside. Most people who do not have a pool think that the heron fishing problem is something of a fancy, and that these stately birds are quite rare and seldom seen in gardens. However, once a pool is established in either town or country the hazard becomes very apparent. Nowadays herons seem quite fearless and will fish quite small pools in suburban back gardens. From their vantage point on high they can easily see the bright reds and yellows of goldfish and orfe and unless deterred will keep fishing until all the sizeable individuals have been devoured.

It is well known that herons wade into the water and stand waiting for their unsuspecting prey. So small mesh netting can be spread out across the pool to stop their antics. Unfortunately this not only looks unsightly, but causes all kinds of problems with the plants growing through it and eventually becomes an awful tangle. The best deterrent is a row of short pieces of cane, no more than 15 cm (6 in) high, placed at regular intervals around the perimeter of the pool. Attach to these a strong black thread or fishing line. When the heron advances towards the pool his legs come in contact with the thread and he will go no further. It is unlikely that he can see it, so he tries from different angles to enter the pool and once again he meets a mysterious invisible wall that catches him just below the 'knee'. After two or three sorties he will almost invariably skulk away.

THE NEGLECTED POOL

Throughout this book advice has been addressed to those who are building and maintaining a pool, but there are many people who inherit a neglected pool, especially when they move to a new home. There is really nothing more disheartening than being faced with an evil-smelling, overgrown water garden and not knowing how to cope with it.

It will depend upon the season as to how it will appear, for a pool of seemingly few plants and crystal clear water in winter is likely to become a tangled mass of foliage obscuring pea-soup thick water in summer. During the summer there may be no water at all, thus indicating a leak. Conversely during winter months the water table in the surrounding soil may be so high that if there is a leak its presence will go undetected owing to the large volume of water around it. Quite clearly then it is the summer when the problem should be appraised, for not only is it then seen at its worst, but if plants are going to be salvaged they have a much better chance of survival and re-establishment at that time.

If the pool is full of water, then this must be drained away before a start can be made. Some older pools made of concrete have removable plugs for this purpose, but after periods of neglect they become difficult to detect. It is most likely, therefore, that siphoning or bailing will have to be resorted to. Siphoning presents no problem when part of the surrounding ground is lower than the pool – see pp. 73–74.

A decision must be taken about which livestock are to be re-introduced to the pool and which are to be discarded. If coldwater catfish are found these should not be reintroduced as they are pugnacious and devour all manner of aquatic creatures, snails and small fish. When they are discovered in a pool they are best removed and given to someone with a sizeable coldwater aquarium. All other kinds of familiar pool fish are acceptable, although it is wise to inspect them all for signs of fungus and white spot disease.

Once the fish are rescued accommodation must be found for the duration of the pool's restoration. The cool of the garage is ideal, and shallow containers with a large surface area should be prepared. Feeding will need to be attended to as the fish will be active and have little to eat, except perhaps for the occasional piece of pondweed. Shade and a large surface area are absolutely essential. Snails must be kept separately, preferably in a large bucket with a quantity of filamentous algae, for if introduced into spartan conditions with the fish they will be pulled out of their shells and consumed as a delicacy. The ramshorn snails are the ones to retain as these feed amost exclusively on algae. They are easily recognized by their flat rounded Catherine wheel-like shells which they carry in an upright fashion on their backs. Pointed snails, especially those of the whelk family should be discarded as they are partial to waterlilies and other succulent aquatics and can be as troublesome in the water garden as land snails are on the vegetable patch.

Neglected pools generally have little variety of aquatic plant life, as the three or four stronger plant species rapidly swamp the less vigorous and usually more desirable kinds. Waterlilies are almost always worth rescuing, certainly if they have mottled foliage. There is no variety of waterlily with blotched or mottled leaves that is not garden worthy. On the other hand be rather suspicious of vigorous large green-leaved kinds as these will almost certainly be one of the forms of coarser varieties. Most waterlilies with horizontal rootstocks are desirable, and any with small rounded leaves and correspondingly small rootstocks should be treasured as these will be pygmy varieties.

Few marginal aquatics are likely to be worth rescuing, but anything with variagated foliage and obvious garden worthy kinds like irises should receive attention. Reeds, rushes and sedges of all species and varieties are candidates for the compost heap, for the likelihood of anything vigorous being desirable is extremely remote.

Floating plants are not likely to be discovered, except in high summer, as they form turions or winter buds and spend the greater period of their life on the pool floor, not appearing until late spring or early summer and then disappearing again in the autumn. The duckweeds often survive but should be avoided as they are particularly invasive and create problems when the pool is restablished. Few submerged plants survive in a congested or overgrown pool. Whey they are discovered there is little point in removing them in their tangled entirety. Short cuttings about 15 cm (6 in) long should be taken and inserted in a tray of clean garden soil which is then stood in a container of water. Be prepared beforehand as many submerged plants cannot survive more than a couple of hours out of water without perishing.

Having saved as much as possible, the remaining mud and debris should be removed and taken away to another part of the garden. Never be tempted to use healthy looking mud for repotting as it will probably contain aquatic weed seeds, undesirable pests like the fountain bladder snail and fish leech, as well as diseases such as waterlily crown rot. None of this affects any of the more conventional garden plants and therefore the mud can be allowed to dry out and be incorporated in other parts of the garden.

REPAIRING A POOL

Few pools that are constructed with a pool liner are likely to survive intact after prolonged neglect and drastic cleaning, although with the rubber variety there may be a case for tackling minor damage. Polythene and PVC pool liners are best removed entirely, even if they look in reasonable condition, and replaced. Vacuum formed plastic and fibreglass pre-formed pools seldom suffer any damage and in most cases will merely require scrubbing before fresh plants and fish are introduced. Concrete, on the other hand, may well have suffered, although it is difficult to assess leakage problems unless damage is fairly extensive. No matter what the pool is constructed of a careful survey of its condition must be made before replanting and refilling can be contemplated.

Pool liners create the biggest headache as they must almost always be replaced. Only where minor splits or damage has occurred to the rubber type, for which there are repair kits freely available, is it economical or even desirable to carry out repairs. The rubber liner is treated in much the same way as a cycle inner tube with a puncture and the repair kit is almost identical to that of a cycle repair outfit. In few circumstances is it desirable to patch polythene or PVC liners – even though repair kits of various kinds are available the repair is likely to be temporary.

Fibreglass and vacuum formed plastic pools seldom suffer damage. It is impossible to repair the plastic kind successfully anyway, but a fibreglass pool that has a crack or severe crazing of the surface can be repaired with the standard motor vehicle repair kit. Repairs can seldom be carried out on the spot, so the pool should be removed and thoroughly cleaned. Fibreglass patching is quite simply carried out in a warm dry atmosphere. Providing that the surface to be dealt with is clean and the processes described in the instructions are followed patiently and diligently, success should be achieved.

Even when a pre-formed pool is not in need of repair it often requires realignment. A pool that is not level can cause problems with flooding at the low end and always looks unsightly when one portion is exposed. It is very difficult to re-align a pool successfully without taking it out of the ground. It should be replaced in the manner described earlier.

Concrete pools, when well built, are the most permanent water garden feature one can have. Properly laid concrete seldom cracks or flakes and is good for many years. Unfortunately the majority of concrete pools are badly made and within a short space of time start to give their owners problems. If a pool has flaked badly with the frost there is little that can be done, except opt for installing a pool liner over the concrete. This can create problems with abrasion on polythene or PVC liners, but rubber ones can often be installed successfully and are reasonably permanent. Fractures in the concrete can be coped with, although it is as well to be aware that any such point is a place of weakness and may be a source of recurring trouble irrespective of the amount of care taken over the repair.

With straightforward cracks, the fracture line should be chipped out with a cold chisel into a 'V' shape. This must be roughed up to allow the concrete of the repair to key successfully to it. A conventional mix of one part cement, two parts sand and four parts gravel by volume measured out with a bucket or shovel is used in cases where the concrete can be allowed to dry out naturally. When this is impossible a quick setting cement can be substituted. The ingredients are mixed in their dry state until of a uniform greyish colour and if desired a waterproofing compound can be added at this stage. Water is then added and the concrete mixed until the agglomeration is of a wet stiff consistency. A good guide to its readiness is to place a shovel into the mixture and withdraw it in a series of jerks. If the ridges that are formed retain their shape the concrete is ready for use.

The old concrete must be soaked with water before the patching is done. Patching is carried out with a plasterer's trowel and smoothed level with the adjacent surfaces. It will take several days to set properly, and even though the repair may look perfectly adequate, there is always the prospect of continued seepage. A wise precaution is to obtain a neutralizing agent and paint this over the freshly concreted area. The free lime in new concrete is injurious to fish and so this is a sensible precaution to take. The most popular brands of neutralizing agent also perform a valuable function in that they seal the concrete by a process called internal glazing. To add further security to the repair a pond sealant can be painted over the new concrete and the adjacent area of old concrete. This sealant is very much like a plastic paint and is applied wih a brush on dry concrete that has been treated with an appropriate primer. The plastic finish is waterproof and a permanent feature of the concrete when applied in accordance with the manufacturer's instructions.

Replanting of relined and pre-formed pools can take place immediately they are ready. Concrete pools on the other hand require a drying out period to allow patches to dry so that they can be sealed properly. Providing that it is a suitable time for planting aquatics, re-establishment can commence.

INDEX